THE JOURNEY

Ida Fink was born in Poland in 1921. She lived in a ghetto through-out 1942 and then went into hiding until the end of the war. Her critically acclaimed collection of stories, *A Scrap of Time*, also published by Penguin, won the first Anne Frank Prize for Literature in 1985 and has been translated into many languages. *The Journey* is her second book and has already been published in seven countries. Ida Fink lives in Israel.

D0877217

IDA FINK

THE JOURNEY

TRANSLATED BY JOANNA WESCHLER
AND FRANCINE PROSE

PENGUIN BOOKS

PENGUIN BOOKS

Published by the Penguin Group
Penguin Books Ltd, 27 Wrights Lane, London W8 5TZ, England
Penguin Books USA Inc., 375 Hudson Street, New York, New York 10014, USA
Penguin Books Australia Ltd, Ringwood, Victoria, Australia
Penguin Books Canada Ltd, 10 Alcorn Avenue, Toronto, Ontario, Canada M4V 3B2
Penguin Books (NZ) Ltd, 182–190 Wairau Road, Auckland 10, New Zealand

Penguin Books Ltd, Registered Offices: Harmondsworth, Middlesex, England

First published in Polish under the title *Podróż* 1990
This translation first published in the USA by Farrar, Straus and Giroux, Inc. 1992
First published in Great Britain by Hamish Hamilton 1992
Published in Penguin Books 1994
1 3 5 7 9 10 8 6 4 2

Copyright © Ida Fink, 1990
Translation copyright © Farrar, Straus and Giroux, Inc., 1992
All rights reserved

The moral right of the author and translator has been asserted

Printed in England by Clays Ltd, St Ives plc

For Miri and Helena

Standing by the window, she thought: If only a star would fall. She was superstitious; in those days everyone was superstitious, each in a secret, private way. She had a great many personal superstitions, but shooting stars weren't among them—to wish on a shooting star would have seemed too romantic, too impossible. Nevertheless, that evening she thought: If only a star would fall—even though it was already late autumn, and everybody knows that stars fall only in summer. Still, she kept her eyes stubbornly fixed on the heavens and suddenly saw a flash of light on the horizon: some careless person had turned on a lamp without first covering the window. This flash in the darkness was not the star she was waiting for, but it could have been, and she took it as a good omen.

Packed inside her suitcase was a horseshoe—really just half a horseshoe, which supposedly broke the charm. She didn't care. She had found the broken horseshoe at the very moment her father was showing her how to get to the cottage of the peasant who was to put her and her sister up for the night. That was enough. She placed her faith in half a horseshoe and an imagined shooting star.

Late that autumn, a dead silence reigned in the ghetto. During the day, not a soul could be seen in the poorest part of town; only in the evening did the narrow, steep cobblestone streets echo with the tired footsteps of workers returning from the quarry. Each night fewer and fewer people came back to the ghetto, and everyone realized that the next transport—the convoy of trucks that would leave the square in front of the public bath—would be the smallest, and the last. It was late, there was no time to lose.

They had slipped out of the ghetto once before, one evening with their father. Protected by the thick trunks of the chestnut trees, they waited by the convent in the blind alley that divided their little town into two worlds. The woman who brought the documents handed them one *Kennkarte*—an identity card—and two birth certificates so new they still smelled of ink.

"And the other *Kennkarte*, for my younger daughter?" Father demanded.

The woman explained that on Elzbieta's picture the left ear was not visible, as the authorities required, and that "without the requisite exposure of the left organ of hearing," the document would only arouse suspicion.

"It's better not to have any *Kennkarte* than a sloppy counterfeit," she added.

Though this made sense, it was also extremely upsetting. Elzbieta had dark hair and an olive complexion. Before, people used to say she looked Italian.

But what could they say to the woman, who claimed

that procuring the documents had not only cost a lot of time and money, but also a great deal of effort and courage, and that they should be happy with what they got.

From the convent came the sound of the bell calling to vespers. They knew the sound well. Every evening they had heard its silvery chime from their house near the river, which, measured in miles, wasn't very far from where they were standing. But now, the distance that separated them from the old house, the river, and the garden seemed vast.

They also knew that right after the bell the organ would start playing.

"There's nothing we can do," said Father. "But these birth certificates . . . they look so new, so fake. Do you really think they'll work?"

"*Panie Doktorze*," answered the woman, "the birth certificates aren't for showing. When you have to show them, it means things are already bad, very bad."

Father didn't answer. He took the envelope with the money out of his pocket. The organ was already playing in the convent. The woman crossed herself, made the sign of the cross on the girls' foreheads, then took from her purse two tin medals of the Virgin Mary and hung them around their necks.

*

None of us had actually been thinking about a journey at the moment when it really began; and yet that moment was accompanied by the hollow rumbling of wheels and the whistle of a locomotive piercing the silence of the night. Until recently, no one had realized that the sounds of the railway station—two miles away—could be heard so clearly from our town, since all the trains used to arrive and leave during the day. But the new era had brought about nocturnal departures not listed on any schedule, and at night the silence amplified the whistling and the dull, subterranean clatter of wheels.

Time and again we stood on the porch, waiting for the signs. It was early spring when we first stood there, our coats still wet from the hours we'd spent lying under the bushes. We were listening to the loud churning of the swollen river—the ice had broken up that very night. We stood on the porch, unable to summon the courage to go back inside, sit at the table, lie down on the bed, resume our normal activities. And that's when the whistle surprised us. We listened to it in silence, it faded and died, and with it faded and died the rumble of the earth. When the silence returned, we knew that the train had gathered speed and entered the forest. That night they took away the elderly, the sick, and the disabled.

After that, we deliberately waited for the whistle and the rumble every time, always standing on the porch facing the river, which we no longer heard because first it was late spring, then early summer, then midsummer, and the river moved lazily and in silence. We heard only the croaking of the frogs and the sigh of the poplars along the river bank.

We stood there for the last time as summer was drawing to a close. Under the canopy of lilacs, the dovecote door was banging in the wind, and the ladder that Aunt Sabina had forgotten to pull up inside or push down to the ground gleamed white against the wall. Cowering in our hiding place, we heard the loud *Raus!* and *Los!* We heard loud, heavy footsteps together with the dainty trot of Aunt Sabina and her daughter Berta.

They took them away at dawn. Why, as they ran with us across the yard, had they suddenly turned toward the lilacs and the dovecote without doves, hidden in the purple shadows? No one will ever know. Nor do I know why I didn't go with Nathan to the *Ostbahn*. I had even grabbed a shovel, the tool of my trade at the time, but quickly threw it down, and instead of running to the *Ostbahn*, I followed the cry "The pigsty, the pigsty!" And I ran to the pigsty, though I knew that it was a pigsty in name only, that it didn't even have a door, that it was exposed to everyone, and consequently useless as a hiding place. As I ran, I saw my uncle drag a half-dead apple tree from the orchard and cover the entrance with its bare branches. Before I crawled inside I looked back: there was the garden with its lights and shadows, shiny and moist with dew.

This time they had surrounded the town in total silence and, using a new tactic, had approached through the fields, meadows, and gardens, slyly surprising us and cutting off our escape route to the countryside and forest.

Later Father said he had been woken by the barking of the dog, so he got up and went to the window. The dog stood in front of his doghouse, with his head up, barking harshly, to warn us.

Outside the window, the landscape lay quiet and calm, as always—the open yard, which hid nothing, lit by the first rays of sun, and further down, the orchard, still in shade, and above the orchard, the steep slope of the castle hill. The dog stopped barking, crawled into his house, and nothing more disturbed the silence, yet Father did not move. Anxiety welled up inside him, he said later, seemingly without reason; he was afraid to step away from the window lest he miss the moment that would reveal the cause for his unease. His eyes moved over the landscape, searching. The birds had just begun to sing, the sky was turning pink. Having scanned the yard, he peered between the trees of the orchard; they stood perfectly still in the tall grass, as if in a painting. There was no warning, no sign, nothing . . . except perhaps for one thing, he said. The crooked branch of the cherry tree overhanging the path suddenly looked like an arm barring the way. It had never looked like that before.

He kept looking—between the rows of currant bushes that led to the riverbank, then up the castle hill. And that's when he saw that the hill was swarming with giant ants. The *Einsatzkommando* was sliding, in formation, down the steep hill toward the river and gardens. Then he cried out, and his cry woke us all.

They were approaching without a sound, their footsteps muffled by the grass, and only when they entered the yard did we hear their boots on the hard ground and on the porch—and then the footsteps stopped. We heard two sharp screams from inside the house, then breaking glass and the slamming of a door. We thought that they had moved on after searching the house, but no, their footsteps once again echoed in the yard, their voices ordered Agafia to open the woodshed and the other outbuildings. They were closing in on us, hidden behind the half-dead apple tree, and when they climbed into the hayloft, they were just above our heads. They had only to look through the gap in the wooden floor to see us huddled in the straw.

One of them jumped off the loft, and stopped in front of the half-dead apple tree. A second one asked, "What's that over there?"

And then a slim pale hand and the sleeve of a uniform slid toward us through the branches. Aunt Stefania put her finger to her lips, as if afraid we might scream, and kept it there long after they left.

As they were leaving, they noticed the ladder by the dovecote.

We didn't yet know what had happened to Nathan. We thought he was safe at work, laying railroad track. But at noon Agafia came and, bending over the gap in the floor, told us. He had run—but had gotten no further than the end of our quiet little street. He was caught in a gentle way, with gentle words. "*Komm, komm, du Kleiner*—Come this way, little boy," said the SS man as he emerged from around a corner. And Agafia, who didn't speak German, repeated clearly "*Komm, komm, du Kleiner*," just as it had been reported to her by an eyewitness.

There was no news about Father. He had been the last to leave the house that morning. As he brusquely pulled on the arm band that said DOCTOR, he had called to us that he was going to the clinic. His face was agitated, and I was struck by this: there was no fear in it, only rage.

Time passed in profound silence, without steps, without voices other than the hushed voice of Agafia, whispering through the gap in the floor, telling us what was happening in town. She had always loved to spice up every bit of gossip, but now she restricted herself to just three words, as if what she had seen or heard had ruined her gift for narrative. "Hordes of people," she would whisper and walk away, only to return an hour later and repeat the same three words.

So the day of the longest and most terrible "action" passed in total silence. Only once, near evening, we heard the voice of our neighbor; she was calling her brother. "Wojtek, where are you?" And we heard his answer from the river bank: "Coming, coming." He was probably lying underneath the poplar tree, just as we used to. Those two voices—nothing more.

We thought that after sundown Agafia would free us from the pigsty, but she didn't. The "action" that had started at dawn was still going on. It was dark when we left our hiding place. The yard, which had shone so pale in the early morning, now shone pale in the moonlight.

Father was waiting on the porch; his face was drawn and angry.

Later, in the middle of the night, he would tell us how he had survived. How he'd been caught and how he escaped. How a friend's wife had stretched her arm across the doorway and, with a clear, wordless gesture, barred his way. How an elderly couple, his patients, had hidden him in their attic. He would tell us all this in the middle of the night.

We were standing on the porch. Our little street echoed with the rapid steps of those who had survived, but the running feet did not stop at our house. We knew that Aunt

Sabina and her daughter, Berta, would not come back, nor would our cousin Nathan. And we were not waiting for them, but for the signs they were about to send us—the whistle and the rumble that would soon reach us in the darkness.

"Hordes of people," Agafia kept saying, reciting the litany of names.

In the middle of the night, Father came to our room, where we were lying fully dressed, our beds still made. The night was windy. In the lilac bower the dovecote door was banging.

"Children," he said, "we have to save ourselves. Fast."

We had talked about escaping several times. But that had just been talk.

This time, I knew for certain, the decision had been made.

*

Once the possibility of a long journey arose—unexpectedly, almost by accident—Father immediately stopped looking for shelter with peasants in the village and turned to Mrs. Kasinska for help in obtaining Aryan papers.

Mrs. Kasinska, an energetic woman with good connections, came to see us on a beautiful day in early fall. In the neighbors' garden they were picking apples.

Father took her into his office and locked the door, and, as we waited for them to finish, we watched the work in the garden, familiar rites and routines that now seemed to us strange and even comical. Nonetheless, we watched avidly, with envy in our hearts, and regretted having to look away when a voice summoned us back to reality and to the business at hand.

Reluctantly, we rose from the porch steps, from which we could see the green orchards in all their splendor, the red apples, the colorful flower beds, all bathed in golden sunlight. Of course, Father's office was also full of sun, but that sun was very different: dim and gray. In the beam that pierced the room, tiny dust motes spiraled. This room, useless now, was rarely cleaned and only the smell of ether and medicines remained the same as before. Sunlight shone on the large bookcase with its many volumes—what secret knowledge we had discovered there!—and on the large Mrs. Kasinska in her flowery dress and little golden curls. She sat in an armchair, smoking a cigarette.

"But they look fine. Just perfect!" she exclaimed when she saw us. "That's a terrific help!"

Father seemed not to share his guest's enthusiasm. Behind his desk, he sat erect, his white-haired head held high, his legs crossed, so that he seemed relaxed, as if he were not the one seeking help. But I knew immediately that it was a false relaxation, just as the polite smile on his face only appeared polite. His face was tense, flushed, and his eyes were unusually blue.

"Mrs. Kasinska is prepared to get the birth certificates and identity cards," he told us in an unfamiliar, raspy voice.

A small mountain of cigarette butts was growing inside the pink seashell. As children, we had often put this shell to our ears to hear the distant murmur of the southern sea from which it had come.

"They look perfect," repeated Mrs. Kasinska, which

was strange because she had known us for years and knew very well what we looked like. But before I had a chance to really wonder, I understood: the way she looked at us, the way she *saw* us now, was different. Mrs. Kasinska had never looked at us like that before, just as I'd never looked at the apple picking as I had just a few moments earlier.

"The most important thing now is to hurry," said Father. "You must understand, Mrs. Kasinska, time is against us. We have to hurry. We've already wasted too much time."

"I understand very well," she nodded, smiling, but clearly she understood it in her way and not in ours. After all, how could she know what time meant to us?

"Well, children, take your pick, choose new last names," Father told us.

He said it the way he might have said, before, in a café, "Well, children, take your pick, choose a pastry." His fingers drummed the green felt blotter on his desk. A muscle in his cheek twitched once, then again.

We were standing by the brown-tiled stove, opposite the window through which we could see the narrow path, known as "the doctors' lilac path," because it ran beside a hedge of lilacs with leaves so bitter and medicinal that people called them doctors' lilacs.

Just beyond the wild, overgrown path was our other neighbors' house, dead and empty since the big "action." The open windows revealed dark, silent rooms. I suddenly remembered the beautiful, olive-skinned girl who used to live there. I turned from the window to concentrate on choosing a last name, but I couldn't think of any, even though I knew many possible names and could have chosen any one of them—in fact, I could have invented a name. And when I did come up with some, none of them seemed to suit me, nor I them. A few even repelled me; I felt that they might do me harm, although I couldn't say why.

Puzzled by my reluctance, Father was growing impatient. Elzbieta was also slow to decide, probably for the same reason I was. But in the end it was she who decided first and said: "Elzbieta Stefanska."

"Wonderful!" Mrs. Kasinska was pleased. Father held out his cigarette case, then lit her cigarette. He looked at me sternly. "And you?"

Once more the long column of names paraded through my mind, passing me indifferently, until at last one name hesitated and stopped in front of me. "Katarzyna Majewska," I said, and immediately pictured this Katarzyna. She had blond, straight hair and clear, radiant skin. My hair was blond, with tight curls, my skin was pallid.

Mrs. Kasinska rose from the armchair and stood facing our neighbors' silent windows. She must have known them because she asked how they were. Father told her.

"And their beautiful, dark-skinned daughter, too?"

"Yes."

"On the river bank she always looked like an Egyptian statue."

And then I seemed to hear again the dark girl's mother's voice, coming from behind the doctors' lilac: "What does it matter that she's so beautiful? What good does it do her? Beauty like that is a curse! Let her have pimples and a hunched back, if only her hair were blond and her nose straight."

We accompanied Mrs. Kasinska to the gate. The street was already in shadow. The sun had set, the gardens were fragrant. The lights were on in the house of the neighbors who had been picking apples. The woman was washing the dishes with smooth, circular motions. I watched her for a long time.

*

The next day we went to the photographer to have our pictures taken for the identity cards. This was the first, essential step, because without special photographs—on which, according to Mrs. Kasinska, the head had to be turned to the right, so the *left* ear was visible—it was impossible to start the process of getting the documents.

There was only one photographer whom we could possibly go to, the one who always took our pictures. We didn't trust the others. They might denounce us, or gossip.

We put on white blouses to look cheerful and on top of them old sweaters to temper the cheerfulness, because we were ashamed to parade around in cheerful clothes. Avoiding the center of the town, we took our favorite path by the river. Willows grew along the bank. The path hadn't lost any of its charm, and this hurt us a little.

Elzbieta said, "Look, it's as beautiful as ever here."

Crickets chirped in the grass; soft, long branches drooped gently from the weeping willows. Under one of the trees sat a group of girls from our school. They were reading some letters. They looked up at us and asked, "Where are you going, for a walk?" but didn't invite us to sit with them. Maybe they were embarrassed, or maybe they were sorry. Maybe they just didn't know what to say to us. Probably they were thinking: What a pity, the Germans will get rid of them soon.

The photographer's cottage was locked and bolted, the walls overgrown with ivy, the yard with grass. It looked uninhabited. But when we knocked, the door opened at once, and there stood the photographer's wife, haggard, her hair disheveled. She stared at us as if we were ghosts. When we asked if we could come in, she nodded, her eyes still full of amazement. The cameras were in one corner of the empty room; covered with sheets of dusty rubberized cloth, they resembled emaciated horses, old and dying. A small child sat on the floor. The photographer, his wife, and the child did not take their eyes off us. Elzbieta whispered, "I can't . . ." and wanted to leave, but I stopped her. Without asking what we wanted, the photographer set up his camera; I sat so my left ear was visible, smiled, and the photographer's wife, twisting her long hair, said, "They killed my mother-in-law, she was trying to escape. I think it was better that way for her. What do you think?"

The photographer clicked the shutter and said, "Good luck."

"Thank you," we answered politely, and he repeated, "Good luck," so there would be no mistake about what kind of luck he was wishing us.

*

Standing by the window, I looked out at the empty ghetto, the narrow, winding streets pebbled like the parched beds of mountain streams, the single-storied whitewashed houses with small, square windows just above the ground. Most of the houses were boarded up, the doors nailed shut forever. Beyond the barbed wire encircling the ghetto rose the garbage heaps of the town dump, and still further was the reedy, marshy flood plain of the river. The foliage, so lush in the upper town, stopped abruptly at the square in front of the former old people's home—the present headquarters of the *Judenrat*—where three anemic trees grew.

Once this poorest part of town had thrummed with feverish life. From behind the square windows came the hum of the seamstresses' and lacemakers' sewing machines, the banging of the carpenters' and shoemaker's hammers. No traces remained of the previous inhabitants. They "left"—this was the word used at that time—in the early spring, during the first "action," and for several months the houses stood empty. When the fall came, human hands righted the overturned tables and chairs, gathered the bedding from the floor. In this way, they prolonged for a little while the last moments of those who had left in the spring, moments which had been frozen inside the looted apartments.

One fall morning, we had left our house by the river. Curtains trembled in the windows along the little street— our departure was being furtively observed. Our handcart clattered along underneath the chestnut trees, carrying the sum of our worldly possessions: the green furniture from the nursery. It was light and plain and easy to transport.

So what if it was useless? We knew that we wouldn't have it for long. Even if our journey didn't happen as planned, even if Father couldn't hide at the beekeeper's, we would simply embark on a different journey, shorter and with no return. Everyone who came into our room in the ghetto stopped in bewilderment at the sight of the green nursery furniture. Sometimes even I would return from work, open the door, and feel as if I were seeing a stage on which the last act of a play was about to begin at any moment.

Standing by the window, I looked out into the darkness. The sun had already set, and the quick dusk of autumn had fallen. I didn't turn my head, I didn't move. I was postponing the moment of saying goodbye. Behind me, I heard Father's footsteps; surrounded by clouds of cheap tobacco smoke, he paced ceaselessly through the room. I heard the gentle click of Aunt Julia's knitting needles. No one knew what she was knitting, but we all knew why. Every so often, Uncle cleared his throat. I felt their presence all around me in this strange room where we waited; I felt their silence, thick with unsaid and unsayable words. The only one whose presence I didn't feel was Elzbieta, because I wasn't saying goodbye to her.

She sat at the small green table, waiting, like me. The room was locked, so no one could surprise us, so no one could discover that we were escaping. The chairman of the *Judenrat*, a stranger to our town, a man who dressed and acted like his masters, had told Father, "If your daughters escape, I'll turn you over to the Gestapo." It was clear that these were not idle threats. How had he found out about our plans, which we had guarded so carefully? He probably just guessed; he knew that staying in the ghetto meant certain death. More and more often one heard stories of Jewish girls turning up in the countryside wearing peasant kerchiefs and sheepskin jackets. We didn't own sheepskin jackets, only old winter coats, which we cinched with rawhide belts to make them look more peasant-like. But our kerchiefs were beautiful, authentic, bought by Agafia in the countryside. They were the most crucial accessory in our travel wardrobe—made of wool, with a long, silky fringe, in a pattern very popular where we lived: roses blooming among green leaves.

That day, the day of our departure, we had each spent a long time in front of the little mirror we hung from the window sash. I saw my face among roses and leaves, against the background of the ghetto—the roses bloomed on the roofs of the empty houses, the branches turned green in the narrow, dead streets. I forced a smile, tied the knot under my chin, first tighter, then looser, pulled a strand of hair out from under the kerchief, then tucked it back beneath the red petals. With each of these tiny changes, the face in the mirror changed completely. I studied it carefully. It belonged to a girl I didn't know, and as I looked at her, smiling, colorfully dressed, I wondered: Which looks better—bangs down, or pulled back? Which looks more Aryan? The suitcase and the bundle contained our new wardrobe—neutral, gray. The pocketbook held our documents: birth certificates, which still seemed brand-new even after we had crumpled them and dusted them with ashes, one identity card, and most importantly a "personal summons" for each of us stating that we were going voluntarily to work in Germany. Elzbieta was being "summoned" by a fruitgrower; my sponsor was a restaurant owner in a small town in Hesse. These documents were issued by the head of the local *Arbeitsamt*—the official work bureau—a Ukrainian. No one knew why he did it. To make some money? To protect himself in the future? Out of some desire to help? We weren't the only ones he had enabled to escape.

Unlike those who'd been rounded up on the street, or those who'd been taken away for forced labor, volunteers knew where they were going and what sort of work they would be doing there, and their documents were marked with a diagonal red line. The "personal summons" had to be stamped at the provincial *Arbeitsamt*. But according to the Ukrainian, this was only a formality. Personal documents, work papers, a prayer book, and half a horseshoe. No money to speak of—just a few zlotys. Money might give us away.

*

I can hardly remember the beginning of the journey. I can recall the darkness of the autumn night, the gusting wind, the rustle of trees in the alley by the convent, but not the walk through the town, and over the bridge we must have crossed—and that's strange, because everything having to do with the river is so sharply engraved on my mind. The first thing I remember clearly is the wide plain opening up before us.

I showed Elzbieta the light in the distance and said: There it is. We were standing on the same spot where, the day before, I had found the horseshoe. Father had pointed out that glimmer of light and said: There it is—and at that very moment I stepped on something hard, bent down, picked up the horseshoe, and put it in my pocket.

"It's good luck, isn't it?" I had said to Father. He paid no attention and pointed again: "There it is," he repeated, adding, "You must not make a mistake."

We ran across the endless plain, along the road of our childhood walks, the road packed with sod from the pastures, smelling of thyme in the summer, the road our family called "the pasture road," though it also had another name, magical and wild: "the Tatar trail."

We ran down the Tatar trail toward the twinkling light. I knocked at the window; the door creaked open. The hallway smelled of sauerkraut and dried herbs. The peasant whispered, "Quiet. There are people in the house. Go to the attic. I'll wake you in the morning."

We lay on the fragrant straw. Ears of dried corn hung from the rafters. The white moon floated across the small window, then disappeared behind a cloud and did not return. We couldn't sleep. Tomorrow, the farmer would let Father know he had driven us to the provincial capital, and then Father would go to the beekeeper's cellar where his bees wintered over in their hives. The beekeeper had removed two hives; Father had bought the vacated space. The fact that we had made it to the provincial capital wouldn't really mean a thing; it would simply serve as a signal for Father to disappear: Father had to disappear at the same time we did.

Don't think about Father in the ghetto, about Mother,

who was no longer alive, about Marian, who had sneaked across the front line. Just keep repeating Marian's words: The craziest plans have the greatest chance of succeeding. Silently, I repeated this sentence once, twice, although I didn't fully understand it. I heard Elzbieta breathing beside me.

We were silent all night. I didn't yet know that from then on it would always be like this: at difficult, critical moments, we would always be silent. Not until daybreak did Elzbieta ask, "What do you think?" and I answered, "I think it will work out somehow." This was another thing I didn't yet know, that she would always ask me this question at difficult moments, interrupting our silence in the shy hope of being consoled, and that I would always give the same reply, not without hope, but superstitiously cautious: "It will work out somehow."

Under the dark sky and fading stars, the farmer harnessed the horses. The thick sheepskin pelts provided good camouflage. The wind made our eyes tear. The horses' hindquarters danced before us. The fields were stiff with frost. In two hours we would arrive in the provincial capital, alone, with only our cleverness to rely on, and our luck.

*

At that early hour, the *Arbeitsamt* was empty. We had come to get our documents stamped; according to the Ukrainian, they would then function as train tickets. The hallway was empty. Typewriters clattered behind closed doors. I slid a strand of my blond hair from under the kerchief, rubbed my cheeks to make them rosy. A stupid smile appeared unexpectedly on my face.

Suddenly, Katarzyna emerged as a naïve, simple country girl, even though I had not imagined her that way at all. Her slow-wittedness appeared on its own, to protect her.

"Stamp please," she said, handing over the papers, gazing blankly at the young German woman. Beside me, Elzbieta also said, "Stamp?" in the same tone and with the same vacant stare. She too had become stupid—suddenly, and on instinct. The German woman, in a red sweater, with red nails and little marcelled curls—my other self, smart and alert, took in everything—smiled at us: two simple girls going voluntarily to work in Germany. The red stripe across the documents said this more clearly than the word "volunteer" written in one of the boxes. She'd already picked up the rubber stamp, stamped the papers, no questions asked, everything in order. It was that fast, that easy.

"You will wait for the transport in the transit camp," she said.

The slow, lethargic Katarzyna disappeared. My voice rose with indignation.

"Camp?" I exclaimed in awkward German, "Transport? They told us we go on our own—no transport."

"Not on your own," she answered, "You will all go together on the transport."

"Volunteers on their own, no transport!"

"Silence!"

A young man entered the room and said in Polish,

The Journey

"Come with me, arguing won't help, those are the rules."

On the way to the camp he made no effort to hide his astonishment. "Why were you making such a scene? Anyways, it's always more fun to travel with others."

But I knew: "camp" and "transport" were bad words. Events had taken an unfortunate turn.

*

A school building, at the entrance to the schoolyard, a guardhouse. Empty classrooms without desks. Village girls camped out on the dirty floor. The room smelled of food packed for a journey: smoked bacon and cheese. Yesterday, a transport had taken fifty girls to Germany, but tomorrow there was bound to be another, because now they were rounding up people from the villages to fill their quotas, and seizing more and more people off the streets.

"So you're leaving voluntarily?" asked the commander of the transit camp.

He sat behind his desk and with his pale, sly face watched Katarzyna, who was no longer a stupid country girl. All of a sudden—who knows exactly when or why—she changed into a polite, well-bred person, smiling shyly. "Careful," she told herself. "This is a sly fox."

"And why are you leaving? Aren't you happy here?"

His fingers were yellow from nicotine. On the desk there was a packet of Juno cigarettes. I would have given anything for one.

"A girlfriend talked me into it. They took her a year ago. She's very happy, she likes her work, she talked me into it. And, as you know, sir—one can see a little of the world."

The foxlike face smiled without taking its eyes off me. I smiled, too. Two well-bred people exchanging casual smiles.

"I see," he said courteously. "You may go back to the waiting room."

"And when is the transport supposed to leave?"

It was too late to unsay those words, which seemed so ordinary and harmless, but betrayed so much haste and impatience. I shouldn't ask such questions. But the transit camp commander saw nothing wrong with it.

"In a day or two," he answered. "We're waiting for more new workers to arrive."

"So perhaps I should go back home and come again tomorrow?"

"Out of the question. Please return to the waiting room."

In the doorway I passed Elzbieta and heard the first question, "Are you a volunteer, too?"

Soon after, Elzbieta returned. She whispered, "I think he's figured it out." There were too many people, we couldn't talk.

By evening, the classroom was almost full. The girls were praying, singing hymns. I sat against a wall, holding the prayer book, my lips moving soundlessly: "Let it work out, let it work out." This would always be my prayer when other lips whispered "Hail Mary" and "Our Father."

Elzbieta knelt with her face in her hands.

The Journey

That same evening, the departure of our transport was announced. Two men entered the room: one older, thin-nish, with a leather jacket and a leather motorcycle cap on his small round head; the other was very young with a pleasant, boyish face, wearing an elegant navy coat and beige kidskin gloves. They walked through the middle of the room, counting the girls camped out on the floor, and then the older one called out, "Tomorrow night."

*

In the morning they took Elzbieta away. She was waiting in line for coffee when someone from the men's transport said loudly, "That one must be Jewish. Just look at her! They must have found some way . . . She should be sent where she belongs."

Elzbieta calmly drank her coffee and went back to the waiting room. An hour later, her name was called. When she left, I lay on my stomach and covered my head with my arms. My muscles went rigid. I lay taut as a string just as I had lain once before when I'd waited for Father. That was long ago, just days after the Germans had entered the city where the war had taken us by surprise. I was living there as a student; Father was visiting a friend. "Last night they took away a lot of Jews," said the maid in the house where I was boarding, and when I called Father's friend, no one answered the phone. I ran out of the house, through the empty streets, to the outskirts of the city where Father's friend lived. On the stairs, I found a man's sock. A white-haired old woman sat at the table inside the apartment; she cried out when she saw me, "They're not here. My brother's gone. Your father's gone. They took them at three in the morning. They're gone, they'll never come back."

Her scream followed me down the stairs. I walked away, calm, icy. The woman whose house I was staying in, a beautiful woman with the face of an actress, said, "Oh God," and tried to hug me. I pushed her away and went into my room. I lay on the couch, covered my face with my arms. My muscles went rigid. I knew I would lie like that until Father returned. An hour later the doorbell rang. He had managed to escape . . .

Waiting for Elzbieta, I listened to the hum of voices above me, the rhythm of steps on the floor where I lay. She had to return.

Silently, she stretched out beside me and covered herself with her school coat. They had wanted to check her documents again. They had asked, "Stefanska? Could that be a mistake, by any chance?" They laughed in her face. There were three of them: the transit camp commander, the man in the motorcycle cap, and another one.

So I lay waiting for them to call Katarzyna's name. But when time passed and no one did so, I allowed myself to hope that the evening—and, with it, the hour of our departure—would come.

In the afternoon we were all ordered to the baths for delousing. We walked through the city four abreast. I didn't like this city. I used to come here once a week for music lessons with a short, freckle-faced teacher. He used to say, "You have to play music with your head, not your fingers." I had never thought about him again, but now, on my way to be deloused, I suddenly remembered him. And I remembered myself in a white blouse with my high school insignia embroidered on its sleeve, in white socks, with sheet music in my hands. But as we returned from the baths, covered with white powder, I wasn't remembering anything. I was busy listening to the conversation of the girls walking behind me. They were outraged because the powder had also been sprayed between their legs. "Shameful," they said, "outrageous." They cursed these hard and shameful times. "This Hitler is a criminal," they said, "but at least he's freed us from the Jews."

*

Late that night we left for the train station. The air was frosty. Stars hung in the clear sky. The loud weeping of the women slowly turned into song. They were entrusting themselves to God. Elzbieta's face was wet with tears. My eyes were dry, my heart filled with stubborn joy.

*

A beam of light shone in my face. I could see nothing beyond that circle of light, aimed at my eyes, which were still heavy with sleep. I had fallen asleep the moment the train started moving.

"What's going on?" I shouted, indignantly. It was how I knew we should sound.

"Papers!"

The bright flashlight made it impossible to see the man standing before us.

"Turn off that light, damn it. What kind of stupid joke is this?"

"Quiet. Your papers—now!"

The light went out. Two men stood in front of us. I was surprised: had the man with the pleasant, boyish face shouted at us? But no, it had been the older one in the leather jacket. The young one just held the flashlight.

"What do you mean, waking a person in the middle of the night, shoving a light in people's eyes! How dare you!" This was how I knew we should sound—and also a way to stall for time and recover from the shock.

The beam from the flashlight illuminated the lapel of the younger one's jacket. "Ladies, please come with us to the next compartment, so we can have a little conversation."

"Don't be so gentle," the older man said angrily. "You have to be tough with this kind."

The car was silent. But just as we reached the door, came the first whispers: "Jews. They caught some Jews."

*

How did I perform that night with the informer in the dimly lit second-class compartment? Katarzyna played her first major role sloppily, amateurishly, because she was doing it by the book: indignant, impudent, rude. And it was all for nothing. I knew that they knew, that they had known from the start, no doubt apprised by the transit camp commander, their fellow informer. I remembered the way they had looked at us as they walked through the classroom, the quick, knowing smile of the younger one.

"Don't be so sensitive," I had told myself then. "Just stop it."

Even though they knew, however, they hadn't taken us to the police; this fact offered some slight consolation. It must be blackmail. They wanted money. But they didn't mention money yet. They said, "Gestapo," or rather, that was what the young one said, the one in the navy-blue coat and beige kidskin gloves, the one who looked like a high school or college student. Sitting alone with me in the second-class compartment, he repeated politely, "Miss, I suggest you confess. Later will be too late. That would be a shame, such a pretty young lady . . ."

He kept his gloves on all night and looked straight at me, always refined and soft-spoken. Only once did an evil gleam shine in his eyes. That was when he asked me, "Why play games? Wouldn't it be better to deal with this like civilized human beings?"

And I answered, "What do you mean, 'human'?"

At that moment, his face changed. His eyes narrowed. He no longer looked young.

"Watch it," he hissed. "As it is, you two are lucky you met us." But immediately he caught himself and remained polite and courteous for the rest of the night.

I knew that my resistance would be in vain, and so would Elzbieta's. She sat alone in the next compartment with the old man, who looked so much like an informer I was embarrassed not to have recognized him at once.

They knew our names, they knew everything. Still, I stubbornly repeated, "No, it's not true," and I offered to go to the police. Then, just as stubbornly, I would fall silent and turn toward the black window pane, which reflected my face, my tangled hair, along with the young informer and his bright kid gloves. And he, with his knowing smile, without taking his eyes off me, kept repeating the same thing. Until finally, after we'd gone through this God knows how many times, he mentioned that he himself might be willing to let it drop because he was kindhearted, but that the old man was stubborn and would never give up. He needed money for vodka and would take us straight to the Gestapo. They paid well, by the head. He added that it wouldn't be the first or the last time he'd done it.

"We don't have any money." I must have sounded as if I was telling the truth, because he believed me.

He was surprised. How could we have set off on such a journey so recklessly, with so little forethought, when everyone knew that at every turn . . . ?

I promised to bring him money in two days. I had no idea how I was going to get it. Then he turned and went into the other compartment to discuss the terms. He wasn't gone long. When he came back, I asked him about Elzbieta. He laughed.

"She is as childish and stubborn as you, Miss. She's sitting there exhausted and pale and keeps repeating her story. 'It's not true. Why don't we go to the police?' And the old man keeps laughing in her face. 'Not true? I know you, you used to buy meat at my brother's store.' You see, his brother sells sausage in your town."

Beyond the windowpane, the light came up, ash gray.

A lake full of gray water appeared. The trees were wet with rain. I remembered that the lake was near the city. We were arriving in Lvov.

"So, we've managed to make a deal after all." The young informer laughed. I had stopped paying attention. The name *Halinka*, which I had been hearing softly in my mind all night, now rang out loud. I clung to it. Halinka was the only person we could ask to put us up for the night. Just for that—we couldn't ask her for money.

When we got off, the train turned out to be empty. The transport had disappeared. I was surprised. I hadn't heard the others get off. Although it didn't make much sense, I felt their disappearance as yet another shock, another loss. We were alone again, in a strange city, without documents and without money. As I clung to Halinka's name, I began to hear another word, insistent and inescapable: *defeat, defeat*. I tried to ignore it, to muffle it, to drown it out: *Halinka, Halinka*.

The informers repeated the name of the street and the bar where we were to meet two days later.

"No money, no documents," said the old man, and they both left.

We stood next to the empty train, on a side track of the huge station in a forest of semaphores and twisted rails, and watched the informers until they disappeared in the mist and the fine, steady drizzle.

*

Four or maybe five days passed between our arrival in Lvov and our departure. I don't know. I can't figure it out, and

I won't even try because it's all so painfully jumbled. Four or five days passed between our arrival and departure from the same (or perhaps a different?) station, between the fine drizzle, in which the informers disappeared with our documents, and the heavy sheets of rain which accompanied our departure, when another informer, rendered harmless, helped us with our suitcase and wished us a good journey. It's hard to reconstruct those days, to push through the nebulous expanses of memory. The fog thickens and thins, the picture blurs and clears. All the bits and pieces must be assembled into one continuous whole, and the task is difficult, and, above all, painful.

After the spies left—the old one in the motorcycle cap and the young one with his beige kid gloves—it's then that the thick fog rolls in. Who knows how long we stood beside the empty train on a side track in the station, or what we said to each other? We must have said something at that moment, when our whole journey was ruined and we didn't know whether we could go on. We must have said something—a few sentences about the night before, at least a few words of despair, consolation, comfort, fear. I can't remember. All I can recall is how naked I felt without my documents in my purse.

The first clear scene is in the streetcar. We stood in the crowd of wet sheepskin coats, inhaling the musty smell of peasant women bringing their baskets to town. We stood in the back of the car, facing the steamy windows. With my fingers, I wiped clear a patch of windowpane. Outside, in front of the train station, was the familiar square, which I pretended not to recognize. There were large, muddy puddles, soggy with dead leaves, everywhere. Wiping the steam off the window, I stubbornly repeated two words: "Halinka" and "money." I barred all other words from my mind, and when they demanded entry, I pushed them away, so that they lodged, aching, in my chest.

The streetcar looped around and traveled along a straight, ugly, treeless street toward the center of the city. Like a pendulum, my hand kept rubbing that patch of window, even though it was already clear.

"Only for two days, Halinka," I would say. "Only two nights. I have to find money for the blackmailers. I will go to my parents' Polish friends, I don't think they'll refuse me . . ." Another hand appeared near mine on the window pane. It was a man's hand—a stranger's. I knew even before I heard his whisper that this hand had appeared for a reason.

I couldn't see the man standing behind me, only his hand beside my hand, which suddenly stopped moving when he whispered sharply in my ear: "If the two of you need help, go to Leon Kicula, 3 Podzamcze Street."

His hand disappeared from the window pane, and I panicked: He's recognized us! We must escape! When he'd said "help," I heard "trap." As the clanging streetcar slowed for the next stop, I made my way to the exit with Elzbieta behind me. From the corner of my eye, I saw the face of a man in a tall sheepskin hat. It was an ordinary face, neither good nor bad, just astonished, and it was this astonishment that made me silently repeat the name and address and doubt my equation of "help" with "trap."

"Remember: Kicula, 3 Podzamcze Street," I told Elzbieta and hailed a black hansom cab.

Halinka lived far from the train station, in a small house in a quiet neighborhood. There was a little park nearby, with shrubs and bushes and trees and other houses just like hers. I had only been there once before, but suddenly I saw it all very clearly: Halinka standing in the doorway saying, "I've wanted to meet you for a long time."

It had been a hot Sunday in early June 1941. The sounds of tennis came from the courts. We were all drinking coffee in a comfortable room. On the table was a vase with mallows; outside the window, a chestnut tree. I didn't remember a word of the conversation, only our happiness— Marian's and mine—and Halinka's indulgent smile. She was much older than we were, divorced. Her face was pale, her black hair gathered in a knot at the back of her neck; her eyes were dark. I remembered her quiet, melodious voice. She worked in a bank. We went home at dusk. "Halinka is a wonderful person," Marian had said.

I had met her only once in my life, but when the war came, and the Germans, I wrote her name and address on my letters to Marian, who did not go to the ghetto but hid in Halinka's house. By then he called himself Pawel, he spent his time locked up in a room set off from the rest of the apartment, translating Shakespeare's sonnets. He also played chess with himself. Until one day he wrote: "I can't sit around doing nothing anymore. We have to fight, defend ourselves."

Then I began to get coded messages about his plan to cross the front line, about new contacts who were supposed to make the plan possible, and about trustworthy people who promised to provide him with guides who knew the way. When he came to say goodbye, in a green hat with a bright green feather and shiny leather boots, he said, "Remember, you can always count on Halinka. She promised to help you. She is a wonderful person."

When we left that June evening, she had said, "You absolutely must come again, soon."

A year and a half had passed, and I was now on my way to see her.

Elzbieta whispered, "Are you sure she'll take us in?" And then, "But who will give us the money?"

To the second question, I had no answer.

The cab driver turned in his seat, leaned toward us, pointed with his whip and said, "Look, the Yids are marching."

On the rainy street a column of emaciated figures inched along. Their wooden shoes made hollow clunking sounds on the cobblestones. I thought to myself that they were probably prisoners from the Janow camp, the one to which Nathan was taken, and instinctively I drew back into the cab.

*

I recognized her immediately. She looked just as she had that day: pale, with black hair, in a dark dress. But she didn't recognize me. She stood at her door; she seemed taken aback. A few moments passed before she exclaimed softly, "Good God!" and pulled me into the kitchen.

The warmth and the smell of fried potatoes made me dizzy. My stomach ached with hunger. I wanted to say that

I wasn't alone, that Elzbieta was waiting in the hall. But she didn't give me a chance to speak.

"So you came," she exclaimed. "Good God, you came. I didn't think that you would dare, and so soon . . ."

I couldn't understand why she seemed so cheerful. Why was she so happy? My heart was pounding.

"I really didn't expect . . . When did you get the telegram?"

"I didn't get any telegram." It was hard for me to talk. Suddenly my lips felt stiff and cold.

She took a step backward, as if for a better look at me. She asked quietly, "So you don't know?"

I shook my head.

"Marian is in the Lacki Street prison."

Fog suddenly filled the kitchen and clogged my ears. I heard my own voice, faint, distant, saying that we had been on the road for three days and that Elzbieta was waiting in the hall. Immediately, Halinka opened the door and said, "Please, please, come in."

I saw Elzbieta enter the kitchen, and it struck me: how Jewish she looked. I went to the sink, turned on the tap, and drank some cold water.

*

We sat in the warm, homey room. A fire roared in the stove. The polished furniture gleamed. On the sofa was an open book, a ball of wool, knitting needles. The three of us sat at the table, eating scrambled eggs and potatoes. Halinka served us sweet ersatz tea, her movements were fluid, graceful, like those of someone in a dream. Perhaps this was a dream, perhaps I would soon awaken.

On the bookcase stood the two glass elephants I had read about in Marian's letters. "Elephants bring good luck," he had written. Marian was at the Lacki Street prison, and I was eating scrambled eggs at Halinka's. Why hadn't I told him to stay?

A week before, the doorbell had rung, and a stranger gave her a scrap of newspaper rolled into a thin tube. On it was only one sentence: "I've been here six months."

"Here," the stranger had explained, "means the prison on Lacki Street." He wouldn't say anything more, and left. A lawyer Halinka knew, a Ukrainian, had more information: Marian was being held as an Aryan, accused of weapons possession, so there was a slim chance.

Six months, and not even a premonition. Nothing. Such a paralysis of instinct. Was it because in his last message he had written: "Everything is going according to plan" and announced that he would not write for a long time?

Halinka said, "I sent you a telegram because I need money for the lawyer who promised to handle the case. I was asking you to send money. Marian's plan was crazy. It couldn't possibly have succeeded. It wasn't my place to stop him, but you . . . He would have stayed with you. He would have listened to you."

I was silent. Warm silence over the glass of sweet ersatz tea. I should have explained, should have said something. But I was silent.

"I'm grateful that you're not telling me to stay," Marian had said, "but if you want me to, I will." That conversation by the dark river, the sigh of the poplars, the murmuring current. My throat hurt, and my heart. How hard it had been to clench my teeth, to not say "Stay." Because staying meant "actions," and the ghetto, and the camp at Kamionki, where all the young men from our town were imprisoned. I was silent.

. Halinka said, "He could have stayed with me until the end of the war. I urged him to have a little patience, but he wouldn't. He couldn't. Something drove him. He used to say, 'The craziest plans have the greatest chance of succeeding.' Is that what he said to you, too?"

I was silent. He had written it to me, and then said it that night by the river. "This plan," he said, "is my own way of fighting back."

"Say something," whispered Elzbieta. Her eyes were large. There was fear in her voice. What was she afraid of?

Halinka said, "You don't have to answer. It doesn't matter any more."

She got up and cleared the table. But before she took us to the room set off from the rest of the apartment, she said one more thing to me. She said it simply, as if it were the most obvious thing in the world:

"Of course you will stay here with me."

*

A dark room, thickly curtained, a kitchen table, a bench, and a bed with an eiderdown covered in red plaid. Against the wall, a chair with a washbowl full of dirty water.

"This is the room he hid in," I said to myself, and

felt nothing. I was numb, weighed down by a feeling of heaviness I couldn't shake off. I was talking to myself—I was always talking to myself—not to Elzbieta, who sat on the bench, just as she would for the next few days, the whole time we were there, motionless, silent, and always with the same expression. I told myself, "It's one o'clock. You only have half an hour. Don't try to think. Just sleep. Sleep will restore your energy and your ability to think. After that, you will have to get up and go look for money for the informers."

Still in my clothes, I slid under the plaid eiderdown; the damp, cold cover made me shiver.

At half past one, I got up, washed my face and hands in the dirty water, put on some makeup, buttoned my coat. Elzbieta still sat motionless, staring straight ahead. I wanted to go to her and say, "You know I won't abandon you." But I was afraid I would burst into tears.

I said, "Lie down, try to sleep. And don't start bawling like an idiot," I added, even though she wasn't crying at all; she just had this pained expression on her face. And that's how it would be between us from then on: no gestures of tenderness. The more we needed to be tender to each other, the colder and more distant we were. Then I left the room, closing the door behind me.

There was a pink lamp over the sofa on which Halinka lay reading a book. Her usually pale face looked rosy; the thick blanket around her shoulders took on the color of the wild rose petals we used to brew tea from at home. The whole room was suffused with a rosy glow. The silence sang in my ears. I stood rooted to the ground, paralyzed by this warm rosiness. I had a lump in my throat. I couldn't speak.

Halinka looked closely at me, and then, without smiling, reached out her hand . . . and now the whole room goes gray. Is it the gray of a rainy day or the gray of forgetfulness? Because I can't remember our conversation. I must have said that I was going out to look for money, that there were only two people I could ask for help; I had their addresses. And she must have said, "Be careful, you lived in this city for two years. It's never been so easy to run into people you know as it is now."

She probably also said that her cousin was prepared to take a letter to Z. Because that evening when I got back, I wrote to Father, asking him for money for the lawyer. I wrote to my aunts, asking them to sell everything we had that could be sold, and I also sent a letter to Agafia, asking her to pass both letters along: one to the hiding place at the beekeeper's and the other to the ghetto.

*

I was on my guard in this city. I was walking down familiar streets, passing familiar squares and buildings, cafés we used to frequent for coffee and chocolate truffles, places of meeting and farewell. I tried to shut out the fragments of remembered conversations, I didn't want to hear them, didn't want to think back. And as I approached a shop window, I saw a stranger walking toward me wearing a flowered scarf tied artfully in a stylish turban, breathless from walking briskly, with a blank and slightly stunned expression.

I was comforted by the sight of that young woman,

like so many other turbaned young women, hurrying home from their offices. No one paid any attention to her, neither on the street nor on the streetcar.

I had almost reached the square with the baroque church, whose magnificent façade could be seen from the windows of the third-floor apartment. In a moment I would be inside that apartment. Surely they won't refuse.

In front of the church, I stopped and took a deep breath. Surely they won't refuse.

The brass plate on the door was engraved with the same name as before; from behind the half-open door, the same housekeeper peered out at me. In a terrified voice, she whispered, "Jesus Maria, you better run away. The family has left the city, Germans are living here now." She shut the door in my face.

In the second apartment a man I didn't know opened the door. I wasn't surprised. I had expected something like this. He said, "Doctor S. died a year ago. His widow is in Warsaw."

So there was no one.

Darkness was falling early. It was drizzling. I forced myself to keep going, step by step; I was exhausted and aching. I crossed the park and sat on a bench by a muddy path.

"No money, no documents," the older informer had said.

I told myself, "You've got to figure something out. You have to get the money. Without papers . . ." But I didn't finish the thought. I was succumbing, more and more, to an overwhelming fatigue. I snapped back to my senses: Elzbieta is waiting, Halinka is waiting, they'll think I've been caught.

I ran out of the park. A streetcar that said PODZAMCZE stopped directly in front of me. Without thinking, I got on. *Leon Kicula, 3 Podzamcze Street.* I was on my way to see a stranger whose address I had been given by another stranger. I realized that the help the man had whispered about would cost a lot of money, but I could no longer think logically. "Maybe . . . just maybe," I kept saying to myself.

Number 3 Podzamcze Street was a dilapidated house on an empty street. There was not a soul around, not even a light. In the dusk I could just make out the distant outline of a freight yard. The house looked uninhabited, but, nonetheless, I entered the stairwell. It was musty; the paint was peeling. I knocked on a door. No one answered. I walked up to the next floor where there was another door with an iron bar and a big padlock. Someone was living here.

A shrill train whistle cut through the silence. Suddenly, terrified by the darkness and the emptiness, I ran back to the streetcar stop. As I ran, I kept thinking, "I'll come back tomorrow. Maybe . . . just maybe."

Now my only concern was to get to Halinka's. A man sitting across the aisle from me was watching me intently. I got off the streetcar and walked through the dark, foggy city, through the gloom brightened only by the yellow glow of an occasional street lamp.

Step by step, building by building. Elzbieta is sitting

on the bench, waiting, Halinka is lying under the pink lamp, waiting. Just two more blocks to the little square, to her house.

A woman in a fur hat looked closely at me and stopped. I kept on walking, calmly, at the same pace.

"Is that really you?"

Immediately, I recognized the voice, the German-accented Polish. Fräulein Hedwig, nicknamed Tschuppi.

In the summer, during our long school vacations, the carriage from the manor would come to fetch the children. The horses wore red tassels behind their ears; though the estate was heavily in debt, the carriage gleamed, and the old manor, with its stately columns and its wrap-around veranda bordering the shady paths, stood proudly in its ancient park. A German governess with a funny-sounding name poured steaming cocoa into cups; she was tiny and round, impish, with eyes like hazelnuts. "*Ach, du mein Liebchen*, my little darling, would you like another piece of cake?" She spoke half in German, half in Polish. She came from Silesia, and there was gossip about a romance with the young owner of the estate who had studied agronomy at a German university.

Fräulein Hedwig, nicknamed Tschuppi. The cocoa no longer steamed on the table, the hoofbeats of the horses had faded away, the manor was first collectivized by the Soviets, and then requisitioned by the Germans. In the fieldhands' quarters there was now a camp for Jews.

"Oh, my dear. They killed Stefan, they killed Frau Lotte, and the beautiful Nina and her father are in a distant town with Aryan papers. Only the young *Herr Professor*, my husband, is here, hidden in our apartment."

And again, "Oh, my dear," and then, after she heard my story, "Don't worry. You'll have the money tomorrow. Both of you will come to our place for coffee. Besides, it's your father's money; the estate was going downhill. They hadn't paid their employees' medical bills for years. They owed your father a fortune."

A miracle had occurred. If I had walked that way a few minutes earlier, or a few minutes later, if that insistent gaze hadn't driven me from the streetcar . . .

*

A fifteen-watt bulb glowed weakly in the room; a huge shadow danced on the wall. I wanted to scream, to laugh, to weep from happiness. Another shadow—Elzbieta's—was motionless.

"Aren't you happy?" If she only knew how close . . .

Elzbieta said she didn't care about anything anymore.

"Did something happen? Tell me."

She repeated Halinka's words: " 'Of course you will stay here.' She wants you to stay—*you*. She doesn't want me."

"Either we both stay, or we both go."

"But you'd like to stay, wouldn't you?"

I didn't know how to reply.

"Do you think that by staying here you'll be able to help him? How? With what?"

Halinka also seemed less than thrilled by the miracle

that had occurred right in front of her house. In the pink lamplight, beneath the fluffy blanket, she kept silent as I talked and talked, still amazed by the encounter that would save our documents. The silence coming from the couch gradually dampened my excitement. I stopped talking.

"It really is a miraculous coincidence," said Halinka in a calm, businesslike voice. "I didn't believe you'd find the money. Your not having any documents would have complicated things—for everyone. But now your sister will go on to Germany to work, and you'll stay here with me. I promised Marian that I would help you. Besides, I believe it's your duty to stay near him."

Listening to her calm voice, I felt that nothing would be simpler than to stay alone in the quiet, cozy apartment and to send the dark, black-haired Elzbieta alone into the unknown.

("Watch out for her, it will be harder for her, take care of her, she is younger . . .")

"I can't stay here without Elzbieta."

"You have to understand . . . two people—it's not the same as hiding one."

"I understand, and I wouldn't dream of asking you to do it. But I can't abandon her."

"She's not a child. She's sixteen years old. Think it over—and you'll see I'm right. If you go, it'll be like abandoning Marian."

"Please understand—I can't leave my sister."

"I'm sorry. It's your choice. You know what I think." Her words sounded so cold.

I didn't have the courage to enter our room. I stood

in the hallway, near the door. Suddenly, I thought: The room is empty, Elzbieta has left. But she was there, she was there. She was still sitting on the bench. She looked at me and knew everything.

"She doesn't want me."

"No."

I stayed up late writing letters to Father, to our aunts, and to Agafia. I slept deeply, and for a long time. When I awoke, I saw Elzbieta, already dressed.

She said, "Don't worry. You can stay. I'm going back to Z. She's right. Besides, it would be stupid to let such an opportunity go by."

(That morning, which had just begun, ends there. There is a gap in my memory, a dark patch. "You can stay. I'm going back." That's all . . .)

At noon Halinka's cousin came to pick up the letters.

"It's nothing," she said when I thanked her for this great favor. "It's nothing for me. I travel all the time. I do a little business on the side—you know what I mean. You have to make a living somehow."

She asked me what sorts of goods were worth taking to Z, what was in short supply there, and what was worth bringing back.

"Elzbieta and Katarzyna escaped from the ghetto," Halinka reminded her.

Halinka's cousin was young and beautiful in her brown fur coat. After she left, the whole room smelled like an exotic flower.

I remember every detail of our visit to Fräulein Hedwig's: how she greeted us in the doorway, saying, "Come in, children," and how that greeting in the hall moved Elzbieta to tears, and how the three of us stood in the dark room amid the heavy furniture, the heavy carpets and heavy curtains, and how Fräulein Hedwig told us that her husband was hiding in that room, that he could hear every word we said but couldn't join in our conversation.

"Say hello to him," she suggested, and politely we said, "*Guten Abend, Herr Professor*," because we had always spoken German to the man who was now in hiding. After our "Good evening," there was total silence—not a whisper, not a breath. Instinctively, we looked around, and with an impish laugh Fräulein Hedwig exclaimed, "Don't even try, don't even try. You'll never find the hiding place, it's extremely clever. It was my idea, I arranged it . . . *nicht wahr, Oskar, mein Schatz?*" I thought I heard a muffled "*Ja, ja*"— but I was just imagining it.

"So now let's have a little coffee. I baked the cake myself." She called, "Oskar, I'll bring you your coffee later." She asked what had happened to the other members of our family, but we didn't know. Our throats were so tight we could hardly swallow the cake. As we left, we said loudly, "*Auf Wiedersehen, Herr Professor*," and Fräulein Hedwig handed us a white envelope.

*

I walked Elzbieta back to Halinka's house and ran to meet the informers. They were both waiting, as we'd arranged, in a restaurant on Grodecka Street. The old one stood at the bar with a glass in his hand; his face was flushed and shiny. The young one sat at a table, watching the door. He was wearing the same kidskin gloves he'd worn on the train.

They counted the money. The old one made a face, as if it weren't enough, even though it was the amount they had asked for.

"Let it go, it's what we agreed on," said the young one. He asked me if I wanted some tea. I checked the documents he had handed back to me and stood up. "I'm really in a hurry," I said.

"I'll walk you," he offered.

"I'm taking the streetcar. The stop is right outside."

He laughed. "Don't be afraid. I'm not going to follow you. I just want to talk to you."

I had the same thought I'd had on the train: Such a nice young man—but an informer, a blackmailer. Probably the perfect informer, precisely because of how he looked and acted. He wanted to help me, he said. My looks were just right, so I had every chance of surviving.

He said, "I have a proposition. Why don't you stay in Lvov?"

In two days, two people—for totally different reasons —had suggested I stay in Lvov, and offered their help. Maybe that meant I shouldn't leave. Maybe it was some kind of sign.

He said he wasn't such a scoundrel. He was a gentleman. First he would rent a room for me, then arrange for a work permit, and later on, eventually perhaps . . . "I'm very attracted to you."

"This conversation is a waste of time."

"Just a second, just a second. Please don't think I'm a professional. I only . . . from time to time . . . with the

old man. I swear. Why should you go slave for the Krauts?
It's dangerous there. There are bombings. You could get
killed. Please think it over."

"I've already thought it over."

"No, no. You have to reconsider. Please believe me,
I'm really a nice person."

I assured him that I believed him and asked him to
please leave me in peace. He wrote an address and a phone
number on a piece of paper in case I changed my mind.

Before I returned to Halinka's house, I went to the
Lacki Street prison. For the second time I said goodbye to
Marian. I explained why now *I* had to leave, why I couldn't
stay at Halinka's. Crying made me feel better.

An elderly man walking by said quietly, "Don't stand
here, my child. Go home. It's dangerous to stand here."

*

Halinka didn't ask what I'd decided, but only looked at me.
Pale and serious, she stood before me.

I said, "I can't leave her. Please understand."

She held up her hands. "You know my opinion. And
you know what I think of your decision."

"I know."

"Leave the key in the hallway, on the windowsill."

"Yes."

"Well . . . that's all. I hope you won't regret your
decision. I wish you both luck."

"I'll send you my address. Will you write to me about
Marian and Father?"

"I'll write to you."

"Thank you for everything. I don't know how to thank you."

"Don't thank me," Halinka said.

I went back to the room and told Elzbieta that at six the next morning we would go to the transit camp from which the transports left for Germany. There was no other way. Then I went to bed. The sheets were cold. I shivered. I tried to fall asleep but sleep eluded me. I could hear Elzbieta crying.

At last the crying stopped, and everything turned warm and bright. "I knew you'd understand," Marian was saying. We were walking down a long, empty street—no houses, no trees, no one except the two of us. At the end of the street was a large red brick building. "No, no!" I cried out in horror, but no sounds came out of my mouth. Then it was raining, and Father appeared in a wet coat, crossing the street with a suitcase in his hand. He said, "This is the only way, my children." I heard him, but he didn't see me. He was speaking into the emptiness—no, he was talking to Halinka, who was standing in the window, holding the pink lamp.

I left the key on the windowsill in the hall and waited, listening for some noise from inside the apartment—the creaking of a door, footsteps. But all I heard was silence. The front door locked behind me with a neat little click, and a pang went through my heart. It was raining outside.

How did I know how to find the camp where the transports left for Germany? Who told me? I don't know, I don't know. Someone must have told me, because we walked without asking directions, without getting lost. In the one image I retain from that walk, I see us carrying our belongings, trudging reluctantly, wearily uphill, along a steep, empty street. Bare trees line the curb.

Later I asked Zosia if she remembered the name of the street on which we found that huge, rambling building, probably a former school. But she knew no more than I did: it was near the central train station, from which our transport later left.

I met Zosia—though I didn't know her name—in that

former school, our second transit camp. I didn't "meet" her, exactly, we didn't exchange a single word, we only glanced at each other, and immediately looked away. She was with a young woman with a flirtatious smile who was speaking Ukrainian and calling attention to herself with her elegant clothes. They were leaning against a bunk bed in a large, crowded room, both pretty and young, one blond, the other dark, and right away I guessed—correctly—that the dark one was a genuine Ukrainian and the blond one, with blue eyes, was Jewish.

"Of course, I remember seeing you," Zosia would tell me later—much later, because at first we avoided each other. "One of the supervisors was with you then, the one with the long neck and the bobbing Adam's apple. I remember him because he took me, too, and interrogated me. But I was able to bribe my way out. I gave him a ring."

I expected from the very start that all our troubles would begin again, and as we trudged up the steep, empty street, I kept trying to repress the thought—as I'd had to repress so many thoughts—that our arriving, unaccompanied, at the camp might seem suspicious and make us the object of unwanted attention.

The guard at the entrance spoke the very words I had feared: "Alone? Not with the group?" He looked at us strangely.

"We are going as volunteers," Katarzyna answered emphatically and a little haughtily. ("Are you crazy?" I screamed at her in my mind. "Why are you talking like that?") And we walked into the yard of the former school, crowded with masses of people awaiting departure, and from the yard into the big room, also full of people who were milling between the rows of bunk beds.

I immediately noticed two young men with shifty eyes moving through the crowd. ("You didn't have anything? A ring? A pin?" asked Zosia in surprise.) But it wasn't until the next day that one of these "supervisors" approached us. He was thin, young, with a long, scrawny neck. "Ladies, may I have a talk with the two of you?" They all must have used the same expression, but our informer in the kidskin gloves had put it more elegantly. He'd said: "a little conversation."

We walked through the big room to a door hidden behind the bunks. Inside was a small office. Beyond the barred window were hills of garbage, refuse from the camp kitchen. A tall man in a slightly dirty trenchcoat, his hat pushed back on his head, stood beside the window. Without looking at us, he lit a cigarette. The thin young man who'd brought us there waited silently.

"Please, go ahead," the man in the trench coat told him, and the other one began, politely, matter-of-factly: Where were you born, please describe your town, tell me the name of the main street, the name of the mayor, the head of the town council, the school principal, the patron saint of the local church . . . We looked each other in the eye like well-bred, honest people. I rattled off names. The informer either nodded, or smiled ironically, at random. He wasn't familiar with the town where Katarzyna was born.

Then he said, "And now, the prayers, if you please."

In the dark room, my eyes fixed on the heaps of garbage, I prayed to God. In a clear calm voice I recited, "Hail Mary, full of grace," and "Our Father, who art in heaven." I answered the catechism questions, and the informer unconsciously assumed the role of a priest refusing absolution: "You say it a little . . . too smoothly."

Then it was Elzbieta's turn, and the whole thing began all over again. The man in the trench coat studied us intently—thoughtful and unsmiling. He looked at us, then at the zealous informer, who was making Elzbieta sing Christmas carols, "Silent Night" and "Gloria in excelsis deo." From beyond the door we could hear loud, angry voices, constant quarreling: "I shit on it, you hear? I shit on it!" and also "You bitch, you were trying to steal . . ."

"You can both go back to the room," said the man in the trench coat.

The informer seemed surprised by this. But clearly the order had come from a superior, because he meekly acquiesced and opened the door for us.

Our neighbors gave us curious stares. A very young woman, in the sort of sheepskin coat people wore in East Carpathia, asked in surprise from the bunk nearest us, "They let you go?"

"Why shouldn't they?"

"Yesterday they took away three girls."

"These two don't look Jewish," another woman said.

"There are some that don't . . ."

The young girl in the sheepskin coat had a round, rosy face and big black eyes beneath carefully plucked, arching eyebrows. She kept looking in her mirror.

Soon after, Katarzyna's name was called. Elzbieta wanted to go with me, but I ordered her not to move.

It was a false alarm. "Someone is waiting for you at the gate," said the supervisor, and I hurried outside. I was happy, because if someone was coming to visit me, it meant I couldn't be Jewish; I was happy, because it had to be Halinka.

Frail, thin, dressed in black, her pale face half-hidden by the veil of her hat, she stood near the entrance. We were only permitted to talk through the fence. Pressing our faces between the iron bars, we kissed.

"Thank you," I whispered. I understood what her coming there meant.

"I was worried. Is everything all right?"

"Yes."

"And nobody . . . ? Nothing . . . ?"

"Nobody."

"My cousin phoned. She got everything done. She is coming back in a few days. I wanted you to know."

I nodded. I couldn't speak.

"Write immediately. Send me your address. I will write to you and let you know . . ."

She would let me know what was happening with Father, and with Marian. She was wonderful. I nodded again, and she said loudly, so that the guards at the gate could hear, "Don't worry, Katarzyna, things are never as bad as they seem."

And suddenly we were both crying, which didn't surprise anyone—in fact, it seemed perfectly natural.

*

When did the man in the trench coat—the one who witnessed our prayers and Christmas carols—when did he approach us? That same night or the next day, after we had returned from the police? Sometimes I remember him coming the same day, sometimes the next day. But he always acts the same way and says the same things. He sits on the bunk, pushes his hat back at a rakish angle, and offers us cigarettes. (Don't smoke, some naïve people had warned us, it may seem suspicious.) As we inhale hungrily, the man in the trench coat whispers so no one else can hear, "You set out too late. Now everyone's on to it, and people are getting caught. It's harder and harder to sneak through, and just two or three months ago it was so easy, no problem . . ."

The man in the trench coat, tall and slim with a weathered, angular face, was the deputy director of the transit camp. He promised to send us off as soon as possible and advised us not to walk around the room too much, not to eat with the others. He promised to bring food to our bunk. And in the evenings, he came and brought us bread with beet marmalade and cigarettes.

("Oh, he was an extraordinarily decent man," Zosia said later. "He helped me, too.")

But he couldn't protect us from the police; his authority did not reach the third floor. He didn't even know that they had taken us directly from the showers and led us through hallways, up and down stairs, to a distant wing of the former school and into a room now used by the Gestapo.

The Gestapo agent sat at a table, and next to him sat an interpreter. Against the wall stood six or seven pale, silent women. Did that older woman and the man with the neatly trimmed mustache lurk by the shower room door every day? Or did they come there specifically to fetch us, after we were denounced by the thin informer who was resentful because he didn't get his fee? Either alternative seemed possible.

*

We were standing with a group of naked women under the warm shower, and the older woman and the man with the trim mustache were waiting at the door. Elzbieta and I both knew at once: they were waiting for us. We saw the looks they gave each other, the looks they gave us.

And we were instantly certain: these were not black-mailers. This would not be "a little conversation" or "a talk." They gazed at us blankly, from under lowered eyelids, and the dullness of their gaze was terrifying. We were instantly certain: these were professionals.

A pale mist in the shower room; the showers roared. Outside the windows, the tops of the trees in the courtyard, a scrap of gray sky, thick rain pouring down. Gray soap, rough as pumice. The room was hot, stuffy, nauseating. I sat on the floor, hugging my knees. I heard the distant sound of a horn; a car was passing on the street. (We used to walk on the streets and listen to honking cars and call out, "A, C, G," and people would turn to look at us.) The giggling of the naked girls, splashing water, attendants with little pumps in their hands, white powder in the pumps. I thought: My legs are pretty and slim. Marian used to say, "You have wonderful legs." I felt the warm floor under my feet.

Elzbieta whispered, "What do you think?"

I knew she was waiting for words of comfort. But, still stroking my legs, I said, "I think this is the end." I didn't know that I would start shouting and that the two of us— and only the two of us—would leave that room in which a Gestapo agent sat at a desk, a woman interpreter beside him, that room in which a group of pale women stood silently against the wall.

I said, "I think this is the end," because that was what I thought. I didn't know then that I would start shouting, "Damn it! I'm not going anywhere! I'm going back home! First they talk you into going, and then they treat you like shit. You can stick your jobs up your asses." I didn't know that, red from the shower and getting redder from scream-ing, I would scream until they told me to leave. I didn't know that we would leave that room, leave the six or seven women standing against the wall, the pale, silent women with horror in their eyes, women whose pallor and silence said more than their birth certificates.

I didn't know then that the sudden wave of despair— this is the end! this is the end!—would come bursting forth in obscenities and profanities, like "ass" and "shit" and "damn it." I didn't know then that this litany of curses, together with my throwing the documents down on the table before anyone even asked for them, that all this would help me more than the best identity card and rubber stamps.

They tried unsuccessfully to put a stop to my outburst. Only when the German jumped up, yelling, "Shut your mouth!" and lunged at me, did I fall silent.

The interpreter looked at the documents and whispered a few words to the German.

"Get out!" he said, and pushed the papers off the table with his riding whip. They scattered all over the floor. I picked them up.

"Come on," I said to Elzbieta.

"What about the other one?" asked the interpreter.

"She's with me," I said.

The hall was empty. The blood drained from my face; the stairs spiraled below me.

*

We walked in the last row, four abreast. Carrying our suitcase and bundles, the informer with the scrawny neck kept us entertained with his conversation. First, he apologized for having caused unpleasantness and problems. "Everybody makes mistakes, don't they?" Then he assured us that "there" things would be fine: "You'll be fine, ladies. Germans prefer the smart ones. It's better to volunteer. They respect people like that."

We were walking to the train station. It was pouring. This was not the thin drizzle that had greeted our arrival, when the other informers left us on a side track of the same (or was it a different?) train station and disappeared with our documents.

We reached the platform, still with the informer at our side. But now he was harmless and, moreover, full of remorse for having hurt the innocent. I think the man in the trench coat went one step—one small step—too far in ordering the informer to carry our things, but it must have been a playful gesture on his part: an ironic farewell understandable only to the three of us.

I felt neither joy nor relief about finally setting out on our journey when everything had seemed to indicate that it would never begin. Perhaps later I would be happy and recall with pride the obstacles we had overcome. Perhaps. But I wasn't sure. The gangly informer wished us a safe trip. Water streamed off his hat.

"Thank you, sir," I answered this contemptible creature, who had asked in such a sweet voice, "The prayers, if you please . . ." I put our possessions in a corner of the car, and then Elzbieta and I stood at the open door and looked for the man in the trench coat so we could thank him. He was nowhere to be seen. From the front of the train we heard the grinding sound of doors closing; the weeping had already begun.

He ran up to us at the last moment. We told him how grateful we were and that after the war, if we survived, we would find him, to thank him again for all he had done for us. Elzbieta gave him as a keepsake a little brass fawn, a good luck charm she'd brought from home.

He smiled, amused. We asked him his name and address. Still smiling, he said, "My name is Kicula. Leon Kicula. I live at 3 Podzamcze Street."

Just at that moment someone shouted, "Watch out,

the doors are closing!" And before we could utter a word, the heavy door of the freight car slid shut in front of us.

A moment later the train started moving.

*

That's how it was. We never got around to questions and explanations. Later Marysia told us that she had come to the train station an hour before it left. One man had guided her, another had smuggled her onto the car; her father had paid an enormous amount of money for her to get on that train.

"Maybe you remember," we kept asking, "was one of those men tall, with a long, angular face? Was he wearing a hat pushed back on his head at a rakish angle, and a slightly dirty trench coat?" She shook her magnificent curls, the color of ripe chestnuts. She didn't remember. Her eyes were the same chestnut color as her beautiful hair.

For a long time she avoided us. She was afraid of Stefa's and Elzbieta's black hair. But then she gave in. The last time I saw her was on a Sunday in spring. We were working on farms, and on our clothes we wore little yellow squares edged with purple and a purple letter P, for "Pole." She came to visit me. She was sad. She said her farmer was mean to her. She left in the evening as the sun was setting. The train was pulling in. Reddish sparks glimmered in her chestnut hair. She hugged me close and kissed me goodbye.

"Why is she hugging and kissing you as if you two were never going to see each other again?" Walenty asked mockingly, after she left.

The German who approached Elzbieta and me had piercing, blue eyes and a heavily lined ruddy face. He was stocky, middle-aged; he wore a checkered cap, boots. He looked at us in silence for a while, then smiled and said, as if to encourage us, "Come with us—our place is really great. First class! *Prima!*"

But his eyes weren't smiling.

Katarzyna shrugged and grinned stupidly. The day was gray. The large transit camp, in which groups of forced laborers were gathered before being sent to work, was drowning in mud and fog. In the square, in front of the gate, a group of young women was preparing to march out.

"It's really great," repeated the German. "Good food, good work, everything good."

We just stood there, which was strange, because we had sneaked out of our barracks in order to leave the camp as soon as possible and get away from the fat boy. Our not moving made the German impatient. With a thin riding whip, which I hadn't noticed before, he struck the side of his boot a few times. But he kept on smiling.

"No," I told myself. "Don't leave. Stay, and take a chance. Perhaps the boy just wanted to scare us. We'll only be here three or four days at the most."

But at that moment I saw the fat boy. He was standing, looking around, in front of the barracks we had just left.

I picked up my suitcase from the mud and Elzbieta grabbed her bundle. Still smiling, the German walked toward the main gate, toward the group of girls.

"Don't leave. Stay. Take a chance," I told myself. But I walked on anyway, and Elzbieta followed. "You can't stay. It's too risky," I argued with myself. We kept on walking.

Someone slammed me in the back, pushing me into the column of women marching four abreast. "Ninety-nine. One hundred. That's it. Let's go!" shouted the German. We marched down a wide road. The German shouted briskly, "*Eins, zwei, eins, zwei, eins, zwei . . .*"

*

This brief scene on the square has stayed whole in my memory, though only scraps and shreds remain of everything that preceded it: the darkness of the freight car and the clatter of the wheels beating into our backs; Darka lying beside us on the floor, decked out with sparkling necklaces and clinking strings of beads; the watery soup at the train station of who knows what city, and the names of two other cities: Leipzig and Kassel. That's all. And, right after that, I see the fat boy standing by the door of the barracks, a typical "blond swine." Hidden in my bunk near the ceiling,

I watched him as he asked, "Has anyone here seen the two Jews who managed to smuggle themselves out of Poland? You should inform the commander at once."

Elzbieta remembered seeing him on our train.

Only later, on the way to the station, did I realize that, if he had really wanted to betray us, he probably wouldn't have made a public announcement. But as I watched him from my bunk near the ceiling, I decided we would not wait our turn, we would not wait until they called our names along with the rest of those being summoned to work at specific locations. We would leave immediately; where we went didn't matter.

On the way to the station, marching in time to the happy German's "*Eins, zwei*," I tried to convince myself that we had done the right thing. I imagined that we had stayed, that suddenly the German transit camp commander appeared and said . . .

But these fantasies brought me no comfort, because I kept wondering whether the fat boy really would have carried out his threat. I wondered whether we hadn't been too hasty to change plans like that and to give up the jobs with the fruitgrower and the restaurant owner in the little Hessian town—for work in some *prima* factory.

Boarding the small local train, I caught a glimpse of the East Carpathian sheepskin coat. Of course, there were many such coats, and many girls were wearing them, but even though I couldn't see her face, I knew that it had to be our neighbor from the transit camp, the one who had witnessed our being taken away for our first interrogation, and later to the Gestapo. It suddenly seemed to me that the further away we got from Poland, the more complicated everything became—nothing was getting easier. We were dragging along all the obstacles we had overcome, and they were spawning new ones, and no sooner did we overcome these than they gave birth to even more. I looked at the young, pink-faced woman, and I could hear her musical, childlike laughter, and her voice, saying, "The important thing is to find a boyfriend." Would she give us away?

I could sense someone looking at me: big blue eyes gazed at me in amazement. I still didn't know Zosia's name. Her look said, "So you're here, too? So we're together?"

They were both here: Zosia and the elegant, flirtatious Ukrainian, Pola, whose name I also didn't know yet. I envied Zosia the safety, the alibi of a Ukrainian friend. I didn't know that Pola would betray Zosia.

The train stopped. It was almost dark. Helping me down from the train, the German said, "*Hoppla!*"

We trudged through the factory town, down the ugly, industrial streets. The people we passed paid no attention. The horizon unraveled in a string of smokestacks; transport labor was nothing new here. Further on, by the river, were long rows of wooden barracks. Streetlights dispersed the thick fog. Dirty, wet snow fell, soaking the barracks. Instinctively, we turned toward them. A voice cried, "Stop! Not that way." One man was leading a hundred women across a bridge over a wide river. On the other side of the bridge, the factory spread out in a semicircle. I tried to catch the smell of the river, but this river had no smell.

"*Das ist die Ruhr*"—that's the Ruhr," said the German. "We are in the Ruhr Valley."

*

We lived in a large room behind the factory buildings. The walls were painted a harsh white; at one end was a scaffolding of double bunks. In the center was a round iron stove. There were long tables and benches, three high windows covered with wooden planks, nailed shut, and three small sinks. Behind the main room was a small washroom which adjoined the commandant's quarters. There was a faint but persistent smell from the toilet, and another peculiar smell which we would come to recognize as the smell of the factory, of machine grease.

This is the background. Everything painted on this background stands out sharply, brightly. The smooth surface shows no spatters, no flaws. But there are question marks. The canvas is riddled with them. Why did he act this way and not that way? And what kind of person was he, after all? How much did he participate in the whole "affair"?

These are questions without answers, because I never asked "Comme-ci-comme-ça," and he's the one I am talking about, the bright-eyed, red-faced German, the commandant of the camp, Johann Schmidt, whom we nicknamed "Comme-ci-comme-ça" so no one would know we were talking about him, though any halfway clever person could have easily cracked our code. (*Comme ci, comme ça* was Johann Schmidt's favorite expression; he used it often, and in all sorts of different contexts.) Perhaps Paraska could answer these questions, but where am I going to find Paraska? And she probably didn't ask him questions like that.

So this is the background to our "affair," which is about to begin, that first evening, without delay, as if there were nothing more urgent. It will start during supper, over a bowl of rutabaga soup, which is tasteless, slightly sweet, and hard to swallow.

Darka was talking to me . . . The beads sparkled against her neck, her green cat's eyes studied me with intense curiosity. And when I heard what she had to say, I laughed out loud.

Just a minute, just a minute. First Schmidt has to deliver his welcoming speech.

In a gravelly voice he talked about the importance of the work we were to perform, about unquestioning obedience and discipline, and about penalties for the smallest infractions. (This was the first time he exclaimed, "*Nix comme ci comme ça!*" and slipping his hand into his pocket with a swooping gesture, he mimed an act of theft). He paced briskly back and forth in front of the group of young women, all but a few from small villages. In their full skirts, jackets, and kerchiefs, they looked at him blankly, not understanding a word. Katarzyna looked at him the same way and didn't move even when, after he'd finished, Schmidt asked, "Who will translate?" and looked directly at her.

Just a minute, just a minute . . . over a bowl of rutabaga soup . . .

The huge kettles appeared and were immediately surrounded by the hungry mob. I hung back and told Katarzyna, "Push, use your elbows, act like the others," when suddenly I noticed a tall woman in a red flannel blouse. She slouched a little, as tall people often do; she had shoulder-length black hair. I thought she resembled a large black bird. I wanted to walk up to her immediately—as if I knew we would be friends—but I wasn't sure if she saw me; perhaps she didn't want to see me.

Someone called out, "Stefa!" and she walked toward a slight woman with mischievous eyes, who handed her a bowl of soup.

I stood rooted to the ground. So there were four of us!

We sat, scattered around the room, each at a different table. This was our first meal together; there was talk of home, family, complaints about the fate that had befallen us. Suddenly and intensely hopeful, I thought, "We've gotten this far, everything will be all right. We'll get along with these girls, our common fate will unite us." Darka came over to me, leaned down, her beads sparkled and clicked. We had traveled all the way from Poland in the same train car. At night she used to cry, homesick for her village in the mountains, and cross herself three times to ward off evil spirits. During the day, she would say, "Let's pray that the bombs don't kill us."

Now her green eyes were deadly serious.

"Katarzyna, dear, I need to tell you something in private," she whispered. "The girls told the commandant that you two are Jewish."

Katarzyna was amused by this, and I laughed raucously, and for a long time. Then I came right out and

asked, "Who said that? I'll go with them to the commandant. Whoever heard of telling lies like that?"

"Some girls saw them take you away to be questioned,
and then to the police."

"So what? They let us go. They wouldn't have let Jews
go."

"Katarzyna, I don't know anything about it, but that's
what people are saying, and not just about the two of you
but about others as well. I just wanted you to know."

"Let them talk, Darka. You can't help people being
stupid."

The girl in the East Carpathian sheepskin coat was
sitting at the next table, seasoning her rutabaga soup with
little bits of bacon brought from home. She was laughing
—a complete buffoon.

Later, we lay silently on our lower bunks, in the last
row against the wall. The room grew empty and quiet. The
straw in the mattresses rustled.

The door latch rattled. It was the commandant,
Johann Schmidt, returning.

"Wake-up time is five A.M. You start work at six. And
now—*Ruhe!* Quiet!"

With my eyes half-closed, I tracked his progress along
the rows of double bunks. He stopped. He had found us
in this dark, stuffy corner. He stood in the aisle, watching.
I breathed rhythmically, softly, pretending to be asleep.
Then there was the click of the light switch, and the sound
of the door being locked.

*

The darkness was noisy with breathing. Someone moaned in her sleep, someone sighed, someone was sobbing. The straw mattresses rustled. I awoke from a hard, tormenting sleep. My muscles ached. My mouth was bitter with the stale aftertaste of last night's soup. In the next bunk Elzbieta was sleeping; her face looked exhausted.

Something had happened, something terrible, but I couldn't remember what. And then, a jolt: they *know*. I could hardly breathe. I got up and, squeezing through the narrow aisle between the bunks, reached the center of the room. I drank some water from the tap, splashed my hot face. It might have been a dream, but it wasn't. I sat on a bench. I stared at the little puddles of spilled soup glistening on the tables. The air was thick, suffocating. Sometime, somewhere, I had sat like this, trying in vain to think.

Be calm, I thought. Don't panic. (Later I would tell myself: Don't be melodramatic!) We have birth certificates, we have documents . . . "When you have to show them, it means things are already bad, very bad" . . . the faraway voice of Mrs. Kasinska . . . in the alley near the convent the trees were sighing, the silvery bell was chiming . . . Sleep. Sleep, I told myself. Think about it tomorrow.

When I got back to my bunk, Elzbieta was not asleep—and she was not alone.

"Imagine, Katarzyna! There's someone here from our town!"

I could hear the anxiety in Elzbieta's voice, though she tried to sound buoyant and happy.

The girl was silent. So I began, "Oh God, from our town! How nice to meet someone from home." My voice, like Elzbieta's, was full of false happiness. Why hadn't I considered this possibility? Who was this girl? If she came from our town, she'd know who we were.

"I was also happy when they told me where you were from." She spoke slowly, deliberately. Her voice was low. I had never heard that voice before. Had she recognized us? Or had she found out where we were from? After all, every conversation began with "Where are you from? What town?"

"What's your name? Maybe we know each other . . . it's hard to see in the dark."

But it wasn't so dark. I could see her face. I had never seen her before.

"No," the girl said. "I don't know you."

Perhaps she didn't want to worry us. Was she being kind?

"I noticed you weren't sleeping, so I came over. I can't sleep either. My name is Helena Pajaczkowska. I live in one of the little houses by the lake."

I immediately saw the lake, frozen smooth, the blue ice we used to skate on after the snow was cleared away. Every day after school we skated past the windows of the little houses along the bank . . .

"My uncle Wasyl has a restaurant on the main street. Maybe you know him. He's my mother's brother. Mama's Ukrainian, you see, and Father's Polish."

This was the moment for her to ask our names and addresses. But she didn't. She said, "I'll move nearer you. It will be more fun together. They took me away just like I was. I don't even have another dress, not even a slip. My mother was supposed to bring a suitcase to the train station, but she didn't come on time."

"Don't worry," we said. "We'll share with you. And you can move over here. There's an empty bunk next to Elzbieta. It will be more fun together."

"You'll share with me? Really? It's so good to have someone from home. They always come through."

I tried to hang on to her last words to quiet my mistrust, but the words slipped away from me. They were slippery, slick, they had no weight.

After that we didn't sleep. When I thought about it, I couldn't make sense of Helena Pajaczkowska's visit. She must have known who we were. Why had she come in the middle of the night? Why hadn't she asked us any questions?

At daybreak I said to Elzbieta, "She knows. She only came to get our things."

*

"Get up!" It was Schmidt. He woke us every morning with the same command. At first he was the only one, then he alternated with Gandhi and Müller. Each called out those same two words in his own way, Gandhi in a nasal bleat, Müller gently, and Schmidt in a sharp, authoritative bark.

The lights went on, and a hundred young women began their morning rituals. An acrid odor of sweat filled the air as the girls sat on their bunks, braiding their hair, tying their kerchiefs, putting on their jackets. Their faces were puffy from sleep. Tin bowls clinked near the huge vats of ersatz coffee, which, like the river, had no smell. There was a long line for the toilet—there was only one toilet.

Schmidt paced up and down the center of the room in his plaid hat and high boots, a smile on his lips, though not in his eyes, which scanned the room, piercing and alert.

I was cooling my face under the stream of cold water for a long time.

"*Na, Katarzyna, gut geschlafen?*" Had I slept well? His voice was gentle, as it had been when he said, "It's great where we're going . . . *Prima.*"

"*Ja, gut.*"

"Do you speak German?"

"*Nix gut.*"

"And your friend doesn't either? Too bad. A few of the girls here know German, and they will get better jobs. I thought you might, too. You both look like intelligent girls."

"*Nix verstehen, sprechen zu schnell.*"

"I see. *Nix und nix.*" He laughed. Katarzyna shrugged indifferently. She was overusing this borrowed gesture.

I watched Schmidt, I saw him approach Stefa. I could hear her speaking fluent German. She was taller than Schmidt, and looked down at him, calm and confident. I thought: She is not pretending to be someone else. She is still herself.

The girls knelt in the aisle between the bunks, each beside her own cot. We knelt, too. Beside me, Hania, another girl from the East Carpathian mountains, was crossing herself energetically. She had a bloated, heavy face, a kind smile, and was very devout. During the night, I had heard her whispered prayers; they had gone on for a long time.

I couldn't pray. I was incapable of prayer. I covered my face with my hands and whispered, "It must work out, it must work out." Suddenly, I realized that the word "must" did not exist in any prayer, so instead I whispered, "Let us survive, let us survive."

We had to go without coffee. We couldn't get near the kettle. And since we had eaten the food meant for breakfast—bread and a little bit of margarine—the night before, we headed off to work on an empty stomach. We stepped outside. It was drizzling and bitterly cold. We sloshed through the wet, muddy snow.

"The new hundred?" asked the guard, poking his bald head out of his shack.

"*Jawohl*, Max, first class. *Prima*."

*

The lights are dim, the machines are silent during the break between the night and day shifts. The factory is napping. It's mysterious, shadowy in the half-light, blurred in my memory, except for a few random fragments—the iron-works, the glass booth above the factory floor, and the stairs that Zosia walked down with the German. The factory does not exist for me as a whole. Was it large? Medium-sized? Small? I suppose it was medium-sized, a munitions factory, manufacturing airplane parts, grenades, ammunition. And it included three camps: the camp where the Russian women lived in their barracks by the Ruhr ("the Russians from the river," we called them), our camp, and the penal camp for French prisoners of war, who were locked up in the factory basement.

In the morning, the smooth-faced young owner would stroll through the factory in his black suit. His hair was black and slick, he carried a black folder in one hand and a pencil in the other. He was always writing things down, checking, double-checking. He looked right through the foreigners as if they were made of glass. The girls used to say he looked like a Jew.

I also remember clearly the moment we approached the factory that first morning, and especially our encounter with the Frenchmen in the yard before the great looming mounds of rutabaga that glimmered in the darkness, the heaps of turnips that nourished both of our camps. They were on their way back from the night shift to their locked basement. They wore the standard prisoner-of-war uniforms; some of them had tied red handkerchiefs jauntily around their necks. I remember them calling, *"Bonjour mesdemoiselles, bonjour mes belles,"* and the girls' delight at finding such amusing boys. Right away there were jokes and conversations in sign language.

Then someone asked a question in French. I guessed correctly—it was Stefa.

"Est-ce que vous êtes ici depuis longtemps?"

The French prisoners immediately turned away from the other girls and surrounded Stefa, and began to *parler, parler* away. Suddenly forgotten, the others watched with envy: "Look at our French girl." . . . "French? Look how dark she is! I wouldn't say she looks *French* . . ."

That moment in the dreary factory yard at the foot of the rutabaga hills is completely clear. I see Stefa, utterly relaxed, still speaking French, as if she hadn't heard what the girls had said.

Again I thought: "She's still herself. She isn't acting.

*

Most of the girls, including Elzbieta, had already gone to work. Only a few were still waiting for their assignment, Marysia among them.

Nothing about the way she looked would arouse the slightest suspicion. She was absolutely perfect, and in the best sense of the word, completely natural, not at all flashy. She had delicate features, thick, lustrous, chestnut-colored hair; her eyes were chestnut-colored, too. What was striking was the winsome, simple beauty of her round, slightly childish face. But I recognized her immediately, and she recognized me, too. She tossed her head and turned away. I could tell she was angry. I watched her sulking; I looked at her delicate profile, her ski boots, her elegant, bell-shaped, light blue coat—later she would tell me, "It was the only coat I had"—and I thought: That's the fifth one, and who knows if she's the last.

A German woman with gray hair appeared in the doorway. "I came to get the one who can draw," she said. Smiling, Schmidt pointed to Marysia, and she walked towards the German woman and said loudly, in high school German: "*Ich bin eine Zeichnerin.*"

Suddenly I thought of Stefa. She was already gone, sitting in the office behind a typewriter.

*

Schmidt led me to the ironworks shop, which was located in a small, gloomy room on the first floor. Several men were working at a long narrow counter that ran along the windows. Machines occupied the center of the room, and at the back, the forge glowed red-hot. Outside the windows flowed the factory sewage canal, full of oily, murky, yellowish water. Later, I would often sneak outdoors to sit on the cement ledge and smell the "river." The stagnant water smelled like a slow-moving swampy river, and I tried to pretend that I was sitting on its banks.

At the sound of Schmidt's loud "*Heil Hitler*," a short man got up from the long table and limped toward us. One of his legs was shorter than the other; that must have been what saved him from going to the front. He was young and strong; his straight, straw-colored hair kept falling into his eyes, and he kept tossing it back with a nervous gesture. He moved quickly, deftly.

"This is Katarzyna," said Schmidt. "She will be working for you. I hope you will be happy with her."

He pulled the foreman aside and whispered something in his ear. Only then did the other one look at me, curious and unsmiling—unlike Schmidt, who burst out laughing.

I will never know for certain what he whispered. But I can see Katarzyna standing there with a bored expression. Once again she acted slow-witted; she put on her armor. I can see the spark of interest in Foreman Glattke's eyes, I can hear Schmidt's indecipherable laugh, and I can even hear his whisper: "They say she's Jewish . . ."

That night I kept asking myself—and Elzbieta—about this whisper. I was sure I knew the words he'd said, though I hadn't heard them.

Schmidt left, and Glattke still didn't say a word. He leaned against the counter with his arms crossed, watching

Katarzyna. The other men were also watching her; they didn't seem unfriendly. They said, "She looks just like a German girl."

Outside the window, the yellow water, the bare wall.

"First of all, we should get acquainted," Glattke said at last, and tossed his hair emphatically. "Why don't you tell me a little about yourself. Where do you come from? What do your parents do? Don't you understand?" Surprised, he explained patiently: *"Vater, Mutter."*

"Vater Bombe kaputt, Mutter tot."

(Our mothers were dead, our fathers were dead, they had disappeared in the war, they had been taken prisoner, killed by bombs. No one cared what happened to us, we had no relatives, nobody sent us packages, nobody wrote to us, only rarely did we get a letter.)

Father was in the beekeeper's cellar, and it would soon be a year since Mother died in that small empty room, in a narrow bed against the wall. Don't think about it, don't think . . .

"Vater Bombe kaputt, Mutter tot," Katarzyna said dully. Staring at the yellow water, she spoke without emotion. She knew that, soon enough, one of the men would say behind her back, *"armes Mädchen.* Poor thing." And indeed someone said, *"armes Mädchen,"* She shrugged again, distancing herself from their pity.

"Do you have a brother or sister?"

"Nix."

"So you are all alone in the world?"

There was no sympathy in Glattke's voice. Katarzyna looked him straight in the eye and, smiling politely, recited her "*Nix verstehen*." Glattke asked no more questions. But he would ask again later—and not just once.

My duties included cleaning the shop, greasing the machines, and sweeping up the scrap metal and iron fillings, which I took out on a little cart.

"The commandant said you are a smart girl, so I guess you will manage."

I grabbed the broom and swept up the fine, glittering dust.

*

During the break I hurried off to look for Elzbieta. I didn't go near her, I just wanted to see where she was.

On the second floor, among the sheets of shiny metal, I ran into Zosia. We stopped at the same moment. No one was around. Her blue eyes looked at me, afraid.

"Do you know that Schmidt has already been informed about the two of you? What are you planning to do?"

"I don't know. Nothing at the moment. I don't know."

"Has he called you in yet?"

"No, not yet."

"There are too many of us here. It's very bad. They know about the others as well. We'll all get found out."

Someone was coming. I said loudly, "What a shitty job," and Zosia repeated after me: "Shitty . . ."

I saw our faces, deformed and grotesque, reflected in the sheet metal.

I found Elzbieta on the fourth floor, beside a mysterious machine that spat out sparks. She sat there, her face streaked with black grease, in the company of other girls also streaked with black. I walked by without saying a word.

*

We returned to the camp for our midday meal. Once again the bridge, the river, the heavy door, the stuffy air. Near the wall a woman, the cook, stirring a large kettle of rutabaga soup with a ladle. Schmidt was standing beside her.

Why didn't he call us in, demand an explanation? Why didn't he say anything?

"He has time," said Elzbieta. "We can't escape, anyway."

"Why?" I asked. "Why can't we escape?"

"How? And where would we go?"

So the word "escape" was spoken on the very first day.

Around the kettle a crowd had gathered, as big as the day before. You needed sharp elbows to get to the rutabaga soup. My stomach burned with hunger, my legs were weak. On the other hand, there was hardly anyone near the sinks—only a few girls washed their hands. Pola was among them, elegant in her ash-gray fur coat, carefully made-up and coiffed; no one would ever think she had just come back from a factory. You could pick her out a mile away. She was different from the others, but not in the way we were. Her good clothes were the only thing that made her stand out from the rest. This difference wasn't a dangerous liability; on the contrary, it inspired admiration and respect. The girls had been trying to play up to her from the very first moment.

Yesterday they were listening eagerly to her complicated life story. She'd been divorced, then married to a *Volksdeutscher*; she had been brought to Germany to work by mistake; she was here in the camp only temporarily and would soon be leaving; a job in a resort hotel awaited her. The girls listened with delight, watched her with delight.

From the very first moment, Pola was the queen of the camp. She was pretty, with slanted eyes, high cheekbones, feminine and charming. Later I would learn from Zosia that she was also sly and treacherous.

Next to Pola was a short, stocky, impish-looking person with an upturned nose. I recognized her: she was Stefa's friend, Paraska. I had seen her the day before. She was vigorously trying to scrub the grease off her hands.

"Damn it, what nasty stuff! I keep scrubbing and scrubbing, and my hands are still black!"

I looked at her in astonishment. Such an excellent face—and such an unfortunate accent!

Paraska was the only one I hadn't recognized right away—not counting the one who hid herself under the huge plaid shawl and whom nobody recognized. Paraska fit in with the peasant girls. It wasn't her high, laced boots, not so unlike our own, nor the long, full skirt, nor her rough gray wool sweater. Was it her walk? Her manner? She came from a remote small town that lay right beside a village—and only her accent gave her away. Still, she wasn't self-conscious about it. She was talkative, she had a sharp tongue, she was the most cheerful girl in the room, almost lighthearted.

Occasionally she used to say, "Oh, you don't know

anything about me," and wave her hand dismissively. And only then did she look like an anxious, worn-out Jewish girl from a small provincial town.

*

That evening, Elzbieta and I were already in on our bunks when Helena Pajaczkowska came over to us. Now I could get a good look at her. She was a shapely blonde with deep-set blue eyes and a pretty but slightly vulgar face. Her skin was oily, unhealthy-looking. I didn't know her. She asked at once about the clothes we had promised her. I opened my suitcase, and Elzbieta untied her bundle.

We didn't have much. We hadn't been able to take much, and anyway, we'd left the nicer things for Halinka to sell. Helena was disappointed in the contents of our bags. She said, "I thought you'd have more elegant things—and more of them." She inspected a sweater and a blouse, tried a dress on, and, finally satisfied, left, announcing that she was moving into the empty bunk beside Elzbieta's that very evening.

Schmidt turned off the light at ten. After an hour, I got up to check on Helena, but she was already asleep. She didn't move next to us that evening, nor the evening after that, nor later. She might as well have disappeared from sight.

We were the ones who, a few weeks later, left our corner and moved near her. But this move had nothing to do with Helena Pajaczkowska—it was merely coincidence that there happened to be two empty bunks below hers.

The Journey

The move was really the result of a series of events that slowly but surely led to disaster.

*

Slowly but surely, our "affair" unfolded; it was no longer just mine and Elzbieta's, but all of ours, because everyone in the room knew about all of us. And Schmidt, of course, knew, too.

The days drifted by—seemingly quiet, benign, uneventful, and yet . . . And yet beneath this placid surface, one could sense troubling undercurrents. There were whispers and giggles too obvious to ignore; sometimes animosity and anger would erupt. Only a fraction of a second separated us from the word "Jew." It still hadn't been said out loud, not once. Still, there wasn't the slightest doubt: we had been found out. The girls were aggressive and hostile to us. And despite all our efforts, the abyss that divided us from the others widened daily.

We were from the city and not from the countryside; we were "ladies," even though we gladly helped out; we washed our hands frequently, brushed our teeth every day. They said: Stefa and Marysia work in clean warm offices, while Pola, who is so elegant, has to work at a machine. They said: The commandant talks to them, he is friendly to them, they've managed to make themselves his pets—he doesn't even look at us.

The fact that there were so few girls from the city didn't help, either. We tried not to stand out, to fit in with the crowd. Perhaps this was our mistake? I don't know.

How can I explain what happened in the weeks that

followed? At the time, we blamed it on the stupidity of the girls who were involved. Possibly they didn't realize that they were passing sentence on us—sealing our doom. Their behavior on the final day would seem to suggest as much. Possibly they weren't evil. But a blind hatred was deeply rooted in all of them, and neither words nor kindness could penetrate that dark jungle of primitive instinct.

*

It was a Sunday afternoon, near the end of November 1942. Elzbieta said, "We made it through November, maybe we'll also make it through December." Elzbieta believed the war would end in January.

She lay on her bunk, her head on a small pillow stuffed with straw and covered with a towel sewn into a sort of pillowcase. Her low, dispirited voice belied her optimistic faith that the war would end soon. She was apathetic. After work she would go to bed and lie there with her eyes closed, or else she would take out the photographs she'd foolishly brought from home and spend a long time staring at each one. She was escaping into the past, escaping back home.

I used to plead with her, "Get up. Sit at the table with the other girls. It's not good to avoid them like this."

But she would say, "I'm with them at work. That's enough. You go."

The girls were gathered around the large stove in the center of the room. This is where they passed their free time: they sang, wrote letters, prayed together on Sunday, and had endless conversations about what it used to be like at home.

"Miss Katarzyna, can you write a letter for me?"

That was the youngest girl in the room, thirteen-year-old Anya, who had come as a substitute for her older sister. She had flaxen hair, a child's small face, and red cheeks, probably frostbitten.

I wrote: "To begin with, may Jesus Christ be praised." I scrawled big, crooked letters, but Anya was, nonetheless, impressed by my skill. She could neither read nor write. There had been no time for school. She had had to watch the cows in the pasture and work as a hired hand for the neighbors.

"And you, aren't you going to write a letter?" she asked.

"I've already written one," I said.

"To your parents?"

"I have no parents. I'm an orphan."

"Miss Katarzyna," she said. "May I ask you something?"

"What is it?"

"They say that you . . . and the other one . . . and one more . . . the tall one with dark hair and—"

"What do they say?"

"Well . . . that you are Jewish." Anya's eyes were blue as forget-me-nots; they regarded me with childish curiosity.

"Oh, they're just gossiping. They've lost their minds. Who would believe such nonsense?"

Anya sighed with relief.

"They've lost their minds. It would be such a pity. You're just like the daughter of the teacher in our village. I don't like Jews."

"But why? They're just people like anybody else."

Anya laughed. "Now *you've* lost *your* mind, Miss Katarzyna."

*

So the seemingly quiet days were in fact full of anxiety and insecurity. We were walking on shaky ground, mined with guesses and speculations. We dissected every fragment of every sentence, every look, every smile; we studied them, as if under a magnifying glass—and we waited. In those early days we felt a growing sense of siege. We wondered: What next?

Schmidt summoned me and said, "Put on your coat and wait at the door. Come quickly!"

"Where are we going?" I asked, and his answer amazed me. "For a walk," Schmidt said—a phrase that did not exist in the camp vocabulary, at least not yet, not until they started giving out Sunday passes. No one had gone for a walk yet. Only Pola got a pass once, and had gone somewhere to see about her hotel job.

"Are all of us going for a walk?"

"Not all," he said. "A few."

I didn't want to take a walk like that, to be set apart with the privileged.

"Let's go—*los*," he said, sharply now.

I put on my coat, tied my kerchief. Marysia stood alone at the door. "And the others?" There were no others—only the two of us.

Marysia said quickly, quietly, "He *would* choose us."

The Journey

The fresh air made us dizzy. Invisible in the darkness, the river murmured. The streets were dim and empty—ugly.

"We don't have much time. *Ein kleiner Spaziergang*, a little walk, a little fresh air." Schmidt laughed for no reason. Or maybe he had a reason. He said, "Tell me, do you like it here? Are you happy?" He hadn't chosen the two of us at random, I thought. No, we didn't like it there. We wanted to go home. We were homesick, we wanted to go back.

Marysia spoke in textbook German; she had studied German in high school. She was wearing her elegant, bell-shaped coat, her ski boots, her handknit, colorful wool hat. "*Ich bin Studentin, ich habe Architektur studiert.*"

And I, with my kerchief tied firmly beneath my chin, in a coat cinched with a coarse leather belt, *nix gut verstehen*. One real, the other pretending, and all of it for nothing.

"You two don't have parents, either?" Schmidt seemed surprised. "So many orphans. Stefanie, the one who works in the office, and her cheerful little friend. They also don't have parents."

In a small, dark store Schmidt bought newspapers and cigarettes, and we bought paper to write letters on, the last thing we needed. The owner asked, "Are you Polish?"

Schmidt nodded. "Yes, Polish."

On our way back, crossing the bridge, we met the Russian women returning to their barracks by the Ruhr.

"See? They can go out alone, without supervision. They've been here a few months. But soon you will also be able to move around more freely. We just have to establish a little order in the camp. Order. There must be order. They say there are Jews in the camp. Several."

"*Unmöglich*," exclaimed Marysia. "Impossible."

"*Juden nix Deutschland . . . Juden Ghetto*," I exclaimed.

"It may just be a rumor, but we have to make sure. Soon this matter will be thoroughly investigated, the documents will be checked. False documents! What impudence! Jewish impudence! They will be sent back to where they came from or else the matter will be dealt with on the spot."

We were standing near the entrance to the camp; we could hear a muffled din on the other side of the door.

"So, did you have a nice walk?" asked Schmidt.

"Very nice."

Marysia and I didn't exchange a word. We each returned to our bunks.

"You know," Elzbieta said, by way of greeting, "they are saying it out loud. Over there, near the stove."

"About whom?"

"Just . . . in general. And what happened with him?"

"He said he knew, and that the matter would have to be dealt with."

I decided to talk to Stefa. But it was she who made the first move. That evening she came to our corner. The snoring from Hania's bunk was so loud that we could talk freely.

"I've wanted to talk to you for a long time," Stefa said.

"Me, too."

"We are in the same situation. And apparently Schmidt knows about us."

"He definitely knows. He said as much to Marysia and me."

"There was also talk about it in the room."

"We have to get out of here."

"I think it's still too early to escape. I have a feeling that things will calm down."

"Calm down? How? He *knows*. Don't you realize what that means?"

"He seems quite friendly to us."

"I don't trust him. I don't know what's behind his friendliness, and it frightens me. Today he told us explicitly that soon this matter would be investigated. That they would check our documents and send us back to Poland or deal with us on the spot. That's how he put it. We have to get out."

"Let's wait a little. I'm against improvising. Get out —and go where? Schmidt has our papers. Escape without papers? We must keep each other informed about everything we observe, and stay away from each other. Let's wait a little longer. And then . . . we'll see."

After my conversation with Stefa, I felt relieved, though I was unconvinced by her reasoning. But Stefa was calm and composed, not impulsive, like I was. Maybe she was right. I wanted her to be right, but I didn't believe she was.

*

The following Sunday, Schmidt distributed ten passes. Among the lucky ones were six of us "city" girls. That was the code word that had replaced the word "Jewish." At first, I wanted to give my pass to my neighbor, Hania, but I didn't. I decided to get to know the area.

Some of the girls went for a walk to the forest. Elzbieta and I went into town. After a while Zosia and Anielka, an ugly girl who wore eyeglasses with thick lenses, caught up with us. Anielka was the only one who, from the very first, had been openly warm and friendly toward us. She was gracious and discreet and never asked us any questions.

We wandered aimlessly up and down the gray, monotonous streets. The city itself didn't interest me, I only wanted to place it on the map. I looked for road signs: they gave the distance to Dortmund and Hagen. The thought that we could escape right then was always on my mind. We were together, we had a little money in our pockets, we had two hours. Who knew when a chance like that would come our way again?

But hadn't I promised Stefa that we would wait? And would it really be wise to escape so blindly, without a plan? No, I wasn't ready—or, rather, I was ready only in theory.

I stood in front of a movie theater and studied a poster: a Wehrmacht officer was embracing a blonde in a backless evening gown. "Run away," I said to myself, but I felt nothing. Not the slightest impulse.

Suddenly, as if she had read my mind, Zosia said, "When you decide to go, you have got to tell me. I'll go with you."

On our way back to the camp we met the rest of the girls together with a group of Polish men who were working for some farmers in the area. I immediately noticed Marysia's flushed cheeks, and Paraska's frantic chattering. The young men gave us curious looks.

That evening Stefa told me that the young men had already been informed about the ethnic composition of our camp: Ukrainians, Poles, and six Jews.

*

Elzbieta shook me from my sleep. In an instant, I was wide awake. Just like when they woke us with the word "action."

It was dark in the room, but no one was asleep. From one of the bottom bunks, someone yelled, "*Zhidivki*"—that was Ukrainian for "Jewish women"—"Go back to the ghetto!"

We lay motionless. Our neighbor, Hania, laughed softly, embarrassed.

"Hania, what's going on? Why aren't they letting us sleep? They should be ashamed. What Jews?"

"Oh, some stupid girl . . ."

"And even if there were some Jews here, so what? They've already suffered enough."

What good would it do to convince Hania, who was one of the quiet ones, and didn't go around poking her nose into other people's business? Someone should have gotten up and said it to the whole room. But I couldn't do it—I was one of those under suspicion. Someone else had to appeal to their conscience, someone whose bloodline and reputation were equally pure. There was no one like that there.

It was Slavka who was screaming, the prostitute from Lvov. Half-dressed, she sat on her bunk, with her large pale breasts spilling out of her open blouse. She was red in the face, frothing at the mouth—that's how hard she was screaming.

Who knows how long we could have withstood this if the door hadn't opened, if Schmidt hadn't come in and turned on the light? Pulling up his pants, with his suspenders still dangling, he didn't look very threatening.

But he sounded it: "Quiet! It's four in the morning! Go to sleep! Sleep!"

After he left, no one laughed out loud anymore. Quiet snickering, muffled by blankets, rippled through the room.

And those laughing whispers frightened us more than the hysterical screams.

*

As if to be spiteful, Glattke had a little talk with me the next morning. He was surprised that I would be so eager to go back to Poland if I had no relatives there. "Poland is my home," I explained. He was scraping an iron bar with a sharp, thin file and, intent on his work, he asked casually, "Tell me, do you like Jews?"

That night I couldn't fall asleep. I kept going over that moment, reconstructing my behavior (had I blushed or turned pale?) reexamining my response, ("I like all people if people good"), and Glattke's easy, dismissive smile. Katarzyna said to me, "You idiot!" And I told her, "It was all I could think of to say." I thought about escape. Why weren't we fleeing? What were we waiting for? I didn't know.

The German women in the office told Stefa that a few Jewish women from the area were still living in town. They swept the streets.

*

Slavka's screaming in the night did not stop with that one performance; it was repeated a few more times, though in a somewhat quieter version.

Not long after, the word "Jew" found a more specific target.

It was late at night. Schmidt had locked us in and had no intention of hurrying back. Someone turned off the lights, and someone else shouted, "Turn the lights on, you Jew!"

The lights went on. Paraska was standing beside the switch.

"I'm no more Jewish than you are. You can kiss my ass," she said.

The dam had burst. The unhappy, hungry girls had found a great topic: Jews.

The most vocal was a small group led by the prostitute Slavka; the rest listened, passively but eagerly, to the stories and jokes. One at a time, each in our own way, we tried to get them off the subject. Some of the girls would keep quiet for a while; others would smile knowingly.

And yet, on occasion, we managed to silence them. Paraska did it one Sunday, when both she and Slavka got passes. She invited her for a beer—who knows what they talked about? But Slavka returned transformed, quiet and subdued.

"I talked some sense into her," explained Paraska.

*

Finally some order was imposed on the way our midday meal was served. Lena, a docile girl with friendly eyes and beautiful, waist-long braids, was appointed cook. She had the bunk next to Helena Pajaczkowska, who claimed that her valuable position near the cook had kept her from moving next to us. Helena, too, worked in the kitchen. She had put on weight and looked even more vulgar.

By then, the issue of food had acquired the importance it had in every camp. We were always hungry. At every meal there were squabbles about second helpings and bigger portions. Lena was fair and did her best; she didn't believe in special favors, nor in sharp elbows. But the rutabaga soup not only tasted awful, it left you hungry an hour later. "Lena, please let me have some of the thick part. Lena, give me more . . ." I never took seconds. My legs shook when I climbed the stairs, Elzbieta was losing weight, but our desire for an extra portion was extinguished by the fear of hearing that dreaded word.

One day, after the meal, I was washing my bowl at the sink when, out of nowhere, Schmidt appeared beside me.

"Have you eaten?"

"Yes."

"Why aren't you taking a second helping?"

"I don't want to. I've had enough."

He looked at me. I knew he understood. "Come."

I didn't want to go. He grabbed my arm and led me toward the kettle.

"One more portion," he ordered.

I said to Lena, "First serve those who haven't eaten yet. Don't listen to him."

"One more portion, immediately!"

Obedient, astonished, Lena ladled some soup into my bowl.

"A full bowl!" he ordered. "Full!"

All through the room, there was grumbling: she went to the commandant to get seconds when some haven't even had firsts.

I tried to avoid Schmidt, to stay out of his sight.

*

The two Germans who alternated with Schmidt at night appeared in the room. One of them was a frail, thin man, stupid and terribly afraid of Schmidt; we had nicknamed him "Gandhi." The other one, in a crooked little hat, with the face of a tired clown, was named Müller. Gandhi couldn't maintain authority, not even for a second; no one quieted down at the sound of his "*Ruhe!*" In fact he preferred joking with the girls to giving them orders and, because of this friendly relationship, he had heard right away about the six Jews. When he looked at us, he knitted his brows threateningly but never spoke. Müller was different. On one of his nights, he came upon all of us near Zosia's bunk. It was late. Most of the girls were asleep.

"You go sleep now," he said—that was how they spoke

to foreigners—"tomorrow you tired." After a while he added, "I know what they think. But it doesn't matter to me who you are."

He didn't say the word "Jewish," and he never mentioned the subject again. From time to time he would bring us a few bottles of good, dark beer. He was shy and funny, with that sad clown face of his.

He talked about it with Zosia, only with her. He fell in love with Zosia and gave her a little pendant with a sheep on it.

*

Once a week, mail was distributed. I waited for Katarzyna's name to be called. Finally a letter came.

Halinka wrote that there was no hope of getting Marian out of prison. The lawyer had taken the money her cousin brought from Z but refused to keep trying. The letter was brief and ended with the words, "Thank God at least the two of you succeeded." Not a word about Father.

I lay awake nights, afraid. My fears for Father and Marian—until then displaced by more selfish worries—were again brought to the fore. The buried past resurfaced, and with it the stirrings of conscience. I couldn't sleep. I felt like crying, but my eyes were dry.

Marysia also got a letter, from her cousin Paulina, who was working for a farmer in the Sudeten mountains. Paulina was doing very well. Her carefully worded sentences made it clear that no one suspected she was a Jew. She'd had no unpleasant experiences, she worked on a farm, it wasn't hard. We envied her. I was thinking about the fruitgrower and the restaurant owner in that small town in Hesse. Paulina and Marysia wrote each other often. All the evidence suggests that this seemingly innocuous fact determined the fate of Paulina, Marysia, Elzbieta, and myself.

*

Illness was spreading through the camp: diarrhea, mysterious fevers, scabies. The toilet was filthy, constantly in use. Urine overflowed into the room; there was always a smelly little puddle near the door. Our ration of soap only lasted for a week—the more frugal girls could make it last two weeks. It was hard and yellowish. The girls said, "Made from Jews."

There were also accidents at work: cut-off fingers, burns. One night they carried Elzbieta in. She had been working the night shift and during a break fell asleep leaning against a machine with sharp teeth which cut into her back when it started up again.

The wound was deep and serious. Schmidt gave me some ointment and a bit of bandage. For a few days Elzbieta lay in bed and then, still in pain, returned to work. She didn't want to stay alone in the barracks. She was afraid of being alone. Every night I dressed her wound, but we had no antiseptic, so that it festered instead of healing.

We weren't terribly concerned. There were other, more urgent problems. The arrival of two Germans in civilian clothes who came in with Schmidt threw us into a panic. They locked themselves in the office and after a while called Stefa in. She came back soon. They had checked her documents, written something down, looked at her in silence. For the first time I saw Stefa anxious and upset.

Soon after that, we left our dark corner and moved nearer the other "city" girls. The only two adjacent empty bunks were underneath Helena and Lena, the cook. Zosia had also moved away from Pola, so now we all "lived" together in the same part of the room. Against all reason, we soon forgot every precaution. Only Marysia still kept up the fiction: during the day she stayed away from us and only came at night to talk.

Each night we gathered on one of the bunks. The other girls were fast asleep. The office door was locked. We crowded onto the bunk, pressed tightly together, discussing what had happened and what we'd observed that day: what Schmidt said, how he acted, who had looked a certain way, made a certain remark. Soon the conversation drifted toward personal matters. By then we knew everything about each other, which in itself was reckless. But it felt good to be together.

We huddled close on the crowded bunk. Zosia was the oldest. Her parents had perished in Belzec. Her husband, a lawyer, had stayed in the ghetto. She kept waiting for news from him, news which would never come.

Stefa was a doctor's wife. She had a snapshot of herself and her husband walking down a country road, both tall, suntanned, a beautiful couple. There were sheaves of wheat in the fields. Her husband was hiding in a village.

Marysia was an architecture student. Her mother had been killed during an "action." Her younger brother had stayed with her father in the ghetto.

Good-humored little Paraska was the mother of a one-year-old boy. She had escaped from the ghetto on his first birthday. Both father and son remained in the ghetto of their small town.

And, finally, there were the two of us. Elzbieta was the youngest of all.

There was one more Jew in the camp. I would get to know her a little later. She joined us at a crucial moment, and then broke away—just in time.

Seven in a hundred. I remembered the words of Leon Kicula: "You set out too late. Now everyone's on to it. You should have left earlier."

*

Christmas was coming. Letters and packages started arriving with the traditional Christmas wafers, best wishes for the holidays, and hopes that this would be the last Christmas in a foreign country. The atmosphere grew festive; things quieted down. The approaching holiday made the girls reflective—and for a while they seemed to forget about us.

A Christmas tree appeared in the room, bringing with it the smell of the forest. Marysia brought tissue and colored paper from the drafting room. We made ornaments, mostly stars and chains. The girls did their laundry, set their hair, and at meals there were long discussions about whether the Ukrainians, who celebrated Christmas two weeks later, should sit with the Poles at the Christmas party. No, they didn't want a joint celebration; a separate table would be set for the Poles, and after dinner everyone would sing carols together.

Elzbieta was irritated by all this holiday cheer. She lay silently in her bunk, brooding, even more homesick than usual. Homesick? "We have no home," I told her. "Stop looking back." It didn't help. Elzbieta brightened up only during our nightly conversations; she felt very close to Stefa. "Let's stick together," Stefa said to her. "The two dark ones."

A German woman from the drafting room invited Marysia to spend Christmas day with her; they would go to church together and then have lunch. "That must mean they don't know in the drafting room, doesn't it?" she asked us, one by one, and we told her, "Obviously not. Otherwise she wouldn't have invited you. Just remember to bring back some cigarettes."

From my bunk I watched the scene near the door. I saw—but couldn't hear—Schmidt and the German woman who'd come to ask if Marysia could have a pass for the next day. Marysia was standing on the side: beautiful, innocent, blushing. I saw Schmidt shake his head and say something to the German. She froze. Afterwards she came over to Marysia—and quickly left the room. "He told her!" I thought.

And a moment later, Marysia, frightened and with tears in her eyes, was saying, "He told her! He told her!"

"How do you know?" I said. "Did you hear it?"

No. She had only heard the German woman cry out, "*Ach, du lieber Gott!*" and then say coolly, "*Herr Kommandant* will not allow it."

He told her.

We sat there, stunned and silent. The smell of the little pine tree filled the air. The girls were setting their hair. Schmidt was circling the room. Why were we so stunned?

There was herring in oil and sweet-tasting potatoes with onion for the holiday dinner. The table was covered with a white sheet. The girls' faces were flushed with emotion; their eyes kept filling with tears. Altogether, there were only fifteen of us Poles. We shared the traditional Christmas host and kissed each other. Once more, I thought: perhaps this shared Christmas Eve, these embraces, will reconcile us, bring us together. At least with this small group . . .

We ate in silence. The herring was salty. One of the girls made a toast with her water glass. "Here's to our being home by next Christmas! Here's to the end of the war!"

After dinner we all sat around the tree, singing Christmas carols—the carols we sang at the home of Tadeusz, a childhood friend; that was why we knew them so well.

"Away in a manger," "Silent night, holy night"—we sang out loud, clearly pronouncing all the lyrics.

Suddenly, amid the singing, we heard someone say, "Let them sing by themselves. Let's see how much they really know."

The chorus fell silent. We kept singing.

Only Elzbieta broke away from the group and ran to

her bunk. She cried loudly, despondently; her sobs filled the room.

*

We had Christmas day off from work. Prayers, Christmas carols, murmured litanies filled the room.

And we thought about the events of the previous day: the scene with the German woman, the episode of the Christmas carols, and another thing we'd noticed during the last few days: Schmidt's behavior toward us had changed. Schmidt himself had changed. He was hostile, abrupt, contemptuous—or else he completely ignored us. You could almost say: now he was acting normal.

The special friendliness and attention he'd shown us before, and which had always made me nervous, was now reserved for the others. In the evenings, he was surrounded by a crowd of girls; he entertained them, joked with them, took the luckiest to the local tavern for beer. The office was always full, and people were constantly finding reasons to go in there. The girls were delighted by these sudden favors from the commandant. They finally had "their man." (The lack of men was becoming more and more apparent, especially in the behavior of certain girls. "Chastity is clearly bad for the brain," the others said. There were also a few lesbian couples.)

Schmidt had a few obvious favorites, especially Pola, who talked more and more about her departure for that job in the resort town.

The loss of Comme-ci-comme-ça's favors didn't bother

us; on the contrary, we were glad that we were no longer the object of envy. The only thing that worried us was the reason for Schmidt's sudden change of heart. What did he know? What did he have in store for us? Did we already have an inkling that not much time was left, that things were shifting rapidly and that these holidays marked a boundary we were about to cross?

"What's going on with you girls?" It was Michasia's soft, melodious voice. "Stefa," she said, "I have to ask you a favor."

Michasia was a slender, melancholy girl with long braids and a pinched little face like a fist. She was the strangest girl in the room. Sometimes she didn't seem quite normal, especially when she laughed for no reason, quietly and maniacally, and when she mumbled nonsense. But most of the time she just seemed sad: silent and abstracted. She washed once every two weeks and never took off the heavy, plaid shawl that covered her head and her back. She knew an endless number of Ukrainian folk songs and sang them in a high, melancholy croon. She was deathly afraid of Germans.

"Stefa," she said in Ukrainian, "why don't you lend me a dress for tonight? I'm tired of these rags. I'll bring it back this evening. Don't worry, I'll shake it clean and pick all the lice out."

"Why do you need a dress, Michasia?"

"Please let me have it, Stefa. I have a pass. I'm going for a walk. I don't want to wear rags—it's a holiday."

She put on Stefa's dress, her coat and shoes. She wound her braids in coils over her ears. Her face, which she'd always hidden under her shawl, took on a new expression; her eyes became enormous. It was no longer Michasia! Full of new spirit, slim, svelte, she twirled around in a graceful dance, calling out, "Aren't I pretty?"

Silent and amazed, the girls watched her.

"When you put on something new, you look like a completely different person," she said, suddenly serious.

Someone burst out laughing. "Different? Different like Jews are different!"

Stefa knew about her; she'd known her before the war. Michasia was Jewish, a Jewish peasant. Skillfully she continued to play the role of a simple, slightly subnormal girl, the incident at Christmas was soon forgotten. But it had scared her, she was convinced she would share our fate. From then on, she kept her distance, and only occasionally visited Stefa in secret, to get the latest news.

*

It was right after Christmas. Dressed in a rubber apron, I was cleaning the machines in the ironworks shop. We're being reckless and stupid, I thought. We should run away as soon as possible, and instead we're sitting with our arms folded, jabbering away. There have already been so many warning signs.

Deep in thought, I didn't notice Glattke, who was standing next to me, watching. He was not exactly pleased by what he saw.

"From tomorrow on, you will be working in the office with Herr Klautz," he said.

I got frightened: yet another cause for envy. "I don't want to," I said.

"Nobody cares what you want. You'll work where you're told."

The office was on the second floor, in a room with windows that overlooked—and was clearly visible from—the factory floor. A glass partition separated the office from the room where the typists worked. So I had Stefa's company. Without moving from my place at the table, I could see her bent over her typewriter.

My work involved measuring samples of steel to be used for airplane parts. I pretended that I'd never seen a caliper before, and for several days I couldn't figure out how to use it. But Klautz, my new boss, was patient: he explained, demonstrated, repeated himself, and eventually I had to understand.

Klautz, who had brown hair and a mustache like Hitler's, made an unpleasant impression on me from the minute I saw him. His pursed, narrow lips and piercing eyes did not bode well. I saw him instantly for what he was: evil, envious, vengeful. He turned out to be extremely demanding and pedantic; he threw a fit about every mistake I made, and when I finally got tired of it and asked to be sent back to the ironworks shop, he got mad and lectured me about the duties of forced laborers in the Third Reich. Luckily, he came to the office less and less often as time went by. He only appeared for inspection and to pick up the measurements, which I wrote down on a special form.

My immediate superior was a jovial, middle-aged German who was soon drafted into the army. I was left alone with a teenage apprentice named Heinz, a little prig from the Hitler Youth. He tried to be mean to me, but I could easily handle him. Then he changed his tune. He confided in me that he was afraid of the draft. What he really wanted was to go the countryside, to his uncle who was a farmer and had plenty of bacon and sausage. He dreamed about sausage.

Sitting at my work table, I could see the whole factory floor. I watched the girls from our camp pushing heavy carts loaded with iron. Their faces were smeared with grease; they wore dirty rubber aprons and wooden clogs. I moved the table so they couldn't see me. But occasionally I had to go downstairs with Klautz and Heinz. Burning with shame, I walked among the girls with my notepad and pencil. They looked at me with envy.

*

One morning I found on my bunk ten days' ration of bread. It was a birthday gift from Elzbieta—I had forgotten that it was my birthday. Elzbieta had gone without bread for ten days, saving it up for me.

Stefa gave me a brooch. That evening, we all ate the bread.

*

Pola, Helena, and a few of the other girls left with Schmidt after supper. It didn't seem strange. Lately they often went out for beer with the commandant. But that evening we heard rumors that Schmidt had not gone with them to the tavern but to . . . a dentist. And a few days later there was whispering: apparently it was not a dentist, apparently they had signed something . . .

Anielka confirmed the rumors. This homely, near-sighted girl brought us all the snippets of information she heard about us, always adding, "I'm sure this will all be cleared up soon, and you'll be left alone." She never forced us to admit anything; she made it sound like gossip and unwarranted suspicion. That day—it was a Sunday morning—she seemed frightened and unusually abrupt:

"I've just come from the kitchen. Schmidt is on his way here with two civilians. I'm afraid it's about you girls. That night they signed a denunciation. I heard them talking. They speak freely around me. But please, I beg you, don't let them know I told you."

She squinted at us with her weak eyes; she was more nervous than we were. Because suddenly, we were quite calm. It had happened. Who would have thought that the code word would be "dentist"?

Schmidt and the two civilians stood in the doorway. Fresh air rushing in from outside made us suddenly aware of how stuffy the room was. Anielka fled. Marysia sneaked off to her own bunk. "Don't let them see us together."

"It doesn't matter anymore," said Stefa, who didn't move.

The commotion had subsided, the room was eerily silent.

"*Ja!*" said Schmidt in a loud voice, "We've come to make sure everyone's here and no one's run away."

The three of them walked through the room toward our bunks.

"This one . . . and this one . . . and this one . . ." said Schmidt, pointing to me, to Stefa, to Paraska, to Zosia, to Elzbieta, and to Marysia, who sat on her own bunk.

"So, they're all here."

They left. The fresh air stayed in the room a while longer. Then it got stuffy again.

"It's not about us," someone said with relief. "It's about them."

*

It had happened. Why hadn't they taken us away? Why was Schmidt suddenly talking about running away? Why weren't we running away? What were we waiting for?

Schmidt was already back in the room. He looked pleased, amused—even generous. He had brought us a large cardboard box full of combs, thread, and yarn. "Don't anybody say they're not treated well here."

What joy! What a tangle of hands grasping at the magnificent gifts! Schmidt ignored the girls around him and loudly called out Zosia's name; she was the only one of us to whom he had never paid any attention. He handed her a large red comb and a few balls of yarn.

Zosia didn't understand what it meant. She asked us why he'd called on her first when he had always seemed to despise her—and especially at the moment when the secret police had just left. "Do you understand it?" she asked.

No, we didn't understand Schmidt. We didn't understand ourselves.

He threw the empty box into a corner and approached

me. "Why haven't you come up? Don't you think you'll need thread?

"*Nix*," I answered.

*

Another long sleepless night. We lay, fully dressed, on our bunks. Through the thick factory walls, we could hear the moan of a siren—all clear. The door lock rattled. Someone was tiptoeing through the room. Who was coming back so late, all alone, and where was she coming from? I didn't recognize her till she collapsed, weeping, on my bunk.

It was Helena. She embraced me. Her breath smelled strongly of alcohol, and I recoiled. "What happened? Why are you crying?"

She didn't answer.

"Tell me what you want or let me sleep—understand?"

"Katarzyna, Katarzyna," she mumbled. "What have I done? I didn't want to. Why did I go? Katarzyna, let me stay with you . . . after all, we're from the same . . ."

I grabbed her by the shoulders. "Where were you? Tell me! Where were you? What have you done? Tell me!"

She pulled away from me and climbed onto her bunk. For a while I heard her whimpering. Then she began to snore loudly. I got up and went to Stefa.

"Pajaczkowska betrayed us. She denounced us. She came back drunk, babbling, and let it slip out. She must have made a convincing witness. I think she knows our last name. I always suspected she did."

From my pocket I took some crumbs of tobacco and

a piece of a newspaper, and rolled a cigarette. It burned unevenly and hurt my throat. "The two of us can't wait any longer, Stefa."

Elzbieta was lying on her bunk. I knew what she was wondering without her having to ask.

"No, no," I said. "There've been so many times when we thought: This is the end. But always, somehow . . . This time, too, you'll see."

*

We were marching to work, four abreast. At the front of the line was Schmidt; at the back, Gandhi. That was something new; until now, one had always been enough. Wet snow was falling, just as it had in November. It was the end of January. Three months had passed.

The factory gate. The guard's shack. The hills of rutabaga in the yard. The muffled clatter of the machines. The high-pitched whirring in the air, and the smell, that unmistakable smell of grease and iron.

I walked slowly up the stairs, stopped on the landing, and looked out the window. It was dark. You couldn't see anything. That was good. In summer it would have been harder, but now, under cover of darkness . . . on the way to work, there was a high wall near the door, and hidden by that wall . . .

Someone called out. Zosia was coming down from the second floor accompanied by a German. It wasn't anyone from the factory. He was wearing a warm winter coat and leather gloves. Zosia was also wearing her coat; she was very pale. A small comb slipped out of her bleached hair, which had grown out, revealing a band of dark roots. I noticed all this in a split second, with that special sort of attention which, at critical moments, focuses on trifles. I thought: She'll have to get some peroxide. Along with that thought came a knot in my stomach. I knew who the man was, and what Zosia's pallor meant.

"Where are you going?" I asked her, and she answered without stopping, "They've asked to see me. I don't know where I'm going, or why."

I ran to let the others know. A stranger was sitting at Elzbieta's machine.

"She burned her leg. They took her back to the camp," the girl explained.

It didn't occur to me then that a burned leg would make our escape more difficult. I was thinking of something Elzbieta had told me a few days before: "Do you know what scares me the most? That they will take us separately."

Elzbieta was lying down. Her leg was clearly wounded, but she assured me that she could walk, even run. She already knew about Zosia. Schmidt had told her, "*Today* they arrested Zosia." It meant that tomorrow . . .

She wanted to go back to work. She didn't want to stay in bed, alone, waiting. Her ankle was red and swollen. How could she put on her shoe?

Zosia returned late that evening. We couldn't believe our eyes. Stiffly, without looking at anyone, she walked through the room, lay down on her bunk, and covered her head with a blanket.

During the night we gathered together. Michasia came over, too. Zosia begged us not to ask her any questions.

She didn't remember anything. She sat wrapped in her blanket, shivering with cold. She kept saying, "Leave me alone, I'm too tired."

They knew everything. They knew where she was from. They knew she was married. She had told that to Pola when they were still in Lvov. Pola had wormed her way into Zosia's confidence, and, foolishly, Zosia had trusted her.

The Gestapo man kept saying: "You're Jewish. Admit it." She denied it. The interpreter—a woman—hit her in the face. At one point the telephone rang. The man interrogating Zosia picked up the receiver. "Yes, yes, I have one of the Jewish women here: Sophie Sokalska. The others' names? Just a minute . . ." From a sheet of paper he read the names. All of them.

"Mine too? Mine too?" Michasia asked frantically, but Zosia couldn't remember whether Michasia's name was on the list.

*

Marysia and Stefa stubbornly insisted on the idea of bribing Schmidt, and this caused our first squabble. Elzbieta and I were against it. We thought we should run away as soon as possible, without waiting till Sunday. What good would a bribe do if the matter was already in the hands of the Gestapo? And what would we bribe him with? We had nothing.

But the majority felt differently. Possibly, they reasoned, we might manage to get some information—find out if they really were verifying our documents in Poland,

and if so, whether the answer had already come. Trying to escape was riskier than trying to bribe Schmidt.

The next morning, Marysia and Paraska gave Schmidt a gold watch, a gold pen, a few gold coins, a chain, and Stefa's boots. They came back looking triumphant. "See? He took everything, eagerly."

This optimism lasted till noon. During the lunch break, Schmidt returned the package to Paraska with the words, "I am not that petty."

The day passed quietly. None of us were called in. This time we decided unanimously that during the night we would work out the details of our escape.

But that very night Paraska came up with a shocking proposal that delayed our escape. Paraska announced that she would spend the night with Schmidt and find out what he knew about our situation.

Laughing as always, Paraska said, "I have something else to bribe him with."

After a long pause, Stefa asked, "Are you that sure of yourself?"

And Paraska said, buoyantly, "Yes."

*

The next morning, Elzbieta painfully squeezed her swollen foot into her shoe and dragged herself off to work. She was afraid to stay alone in the camp. The girls had suddenly become excited about an incident that had occurred in Frankfurt: several Jewish women with Aryan papers had been hanged. One was saved by a petition with ten signatures stating that she was a genuine Pole.

Were these just sadistic rumors meant to frighten us? Who knows? How could we have gathered ten signatures in our camp? Anielka would certainly have signed, and perhaps also Hania, our former neighbor. But not long before, Hania had said to me, "If it's true that you're Jewish, I'm surprised you're not afraid to lie like this. Lying's such a terrible sin . . ."

I was anxious at work, and to make things worse, Heinz was bothering me with *his* troubles: he was going to be drafted. "Are they sending children off to war?" I asked him. He was so distracted that he didn't catch my sarcasm. I sat with my back to the door, and every time the door creaked, my heart began to pound. I caught Stefa's eye. Bent over her typewriter, stooped even more than usual, she kept glancing in my direction. What would Paraska's night with Schmidt bring us?

During the lunch break, no one mentioned the Jews in Frankfurt: the big news was that Helena Pajaczkowska had been promoted to switchboard operator. In addition to her headset, she was sporting a new dress and a new sweater.

*

Paraska kept her promise. That night, at eleven, Schmidt was waiting for her in his room. She borrowed a nightgown from Marysia. She was very nervous and kept saying that she was sacrificing herself for us. It sounded funny, but no one laughed.

"Remember," we said, "we're all in this together. It's not just you."

"Don't worry," she assured us. "I remember."

We went to bed early. At ten Schmidt turned off the lights. The conversations grew quieter, then stopped. Everyone in the room fell asleep. Paraska gingerly opened the door to the washroom which separated our bunks from the commandant's room. In the bright wedge of light we saw, in silhouette, Paraska in her long nightgown. Then the door closed.

An hour passed. Two hours. Exhausted by the tension, I fell soundly asleep. I was awoken by Elzbieta's whisper: "She's back." I crept toward Stefa. On the next bunk lay Paraska, fast asleep. Stefa didn't know any details. Paraska had promised to talk about it in the morning.

On the way to the factory, Stefa whispered, "I'll tell you in the office." There was no time to ask whether the news was good or bad.

Nervously, hurriedly, I filled out the forms, wrote down the measurements. Klautz was surprised by my diligence. "Usually, you're so damn lazy." I couldn't wait for him to leave the room. The moment the door closed behind him, Stefa ran in.

Paraska's report, as relayed by Stefa, was short and concise. Schmidt had said that we still had time; he would tell us when we had to escape, on what day and at what hour. Paraska trusted him completely. She had talked to him frankly, without mincing words.

Stefa also added that Schmidt knew Elzbieta's and my last name—and that we were sisters.

*

That very evening the news hit us like a bombshell: On Thursday, January 29, we would be taken away. It wasn't clear who started the rumor; it appeared out of nowhere and was soon being whispered, from person to person, around the room. The girls were also discussing the fact that Pola had been released from the camp and was about to leave for her job in the resort hotel.

It was Saturday. Thursday was five days away. Paraska again spent the night with Schmidt, who, just as he had the night before, advised us to wait; he would let us know.

We lay on our bunks, waiting.

Sunday. No passes. The girls were sewing, writing letters, singing. On past Sundays we had joined in; singing brought relief, it was a substitute for screaming. But that day no one had any desire to sing.

We lay on our bunks, waiting.

In the evening, Schmidt brought in a young man with an accordion. We easily recognized him as a foreigner, though he didn't say a word. He just stared straight ahead with a sleepy, heavy-lidded look. Schmidt ordered him to sit near the wall and announced loudly, pointedly:

"See, we even provide entertainment for you. There will be dancing tonight."

We couldn't believe our ears. Dancing? The musician struck up a lively tune, and soon everybody was dancing.

"Come on," I said to Marysia. "We have to keep playing our parts." Even Elzbieta dragged herself off her bunk and, limping, danced with Stefa. Suddenly it seemed to get quieter and less crowded; the center of the room cleared out. The girls stood against the wall, whispering among themselves. Among the dancing couples was Schmidt and Paraska.

"He's dancing with the Jew," whispered the girls. "But she won't be dancing much longer."

The music stopped. The accordion player wiped his sweaty brow. Just then, the girls started singing a song called "The Last Sunday," first shyly and tentatively, then louder and louder. They gathered in a little group and sang even louder and more boldly.

"Listen!" someone shouted, "we're singing for you! This is your last Sunday!"

I thought: I still have a piece of soap. I'll sell it. I have to smoke. I wanted a cigarette more than anything else in the world.

"How many cigarettes will you give me?"

"Five."

"Give me ten!"

"Seven."

"Fine. Seven."

I inhaled greedily, and everything started spinning. "All right," I called out, "Marysia, Zosia, Elzbieta, Paraska—let's sing! All together! We'll drown them out!

> "Today is our last Sunday,
> Don't keep your love from me,
> Gaze at me tenderly
> This one last time . . ."

Zosia couldn't stand it. She ran away to her bunk and covered herself with her blanket. Stefa's face was pale and

bloodless. Marysia's lips were trembling from holding back
a moan. But we kept singing:

> *"Oh, give me this one Sunday,*
> *This one last Sunday,*
> *Then let the world just end."*

The room swam before my eyes. The sweaty faces of
the girls became one big blur; their mouths merged into
one open mouth singing *"Sunday . . . our last Sunday!"*
The singing turned to yelling, they spat out the words,
choked with laughter, stamped their feet. They were not
the same girls who had first come here with us. They were
hysterical.

The accordion player didn't move from his chair. His
eyes filled with horror. He kept trying to play different tunes
but a hundred healthy voices drowned him out, as the girls
maniacally repeated this one song.

"What's going on here?" Schmidt's shout rose above
the noise. And all at once, the girls fell absolutely silent—
that was how much control he had.

From out of the crowd Pola spoke up in her soft,
melodious accent: "We are singing a Polish tango called
'The Last Sunday.'" And she laughed a brief, sensual laugh.

*

Monday. Klautz was having a fit. The latest measurements
were full of mistakes. He screamed, "This looks like sab-
otage. You had better not be insolent, you . . . you . . .
Watch out. I'm warning you."

Tuesday. I was in the office. Stefa hadn't come in yet.

I looked worriedly at the empty seat in front of her type-writer. She had left the barracks with the others. That was an hour ago, and she still wasn't here. Finally she arrived. Her face was frozen, masklike. She was extremely pale and didn't look in my direction.

You have to come and tell me, I pleaded with her silently. Now, right away, get up and come . . .

As if obeying my thoughts, she got up and was soon beside me. I saw the look on her face—and suddenly I was worried about Elzbieta. She said, "Schmidt told Paraska she should be ready to leave tonight."

"What do you mean *Paraska*?" My voice was hoarse.

"He wants to help Paraska—and me, because I'm her best friend. Just us."

I couldn't speak. We looked each other in the eye.

She said, "I know, I know. We agreed we all had to leave together, at the same time. But he doesn't want . . . he . . ."

"I understand. It's fine." My voice had returned to normal. "It's wonderful that he wants to help you."

"You must understand. Please try to understand."

"I do understand."

"Get back here, please." A voice called from the other room.

"All of you have to run away, too, as soon as possible," said Stefa on her way out.

In front of me lay the narrow strips of aluminum. I measured them, tallying the numbers, marking the strips with blue chalk. From the corner of my eye I could see Stefa, bent over, resting her head on her hand, gazing out the window. Dirty wet snow was falling outside. It fell and fell, without leaving a trace. It would fall throughout the night. We all had to leave together. If just one of us escaped it would endanger the others. We were all under suspicion. We had to run away together. I remembered Paraska's words: "I'm sacrificing myself for everybody . . . I'm not doing this for myself."

Everything was fine. After all, it was Paraska who had slept with Schmidt, and Stefa was her friend, and so everything was fine. Everything was as it should be. I couldn't count straight. I knew only one thing: we couldn't stay in the camp after Paraska and Stefa disappeared. We had to run away that very night.

We looked at each other through the glass wall. She was already on the other side—safe.

She must have read something in my eyes, because she jumped up from her chair and, ignoring the German woman, who was calling after her, ran into my office. "You blame us, don't you?"

"No, I don't. I understand."

I should have embraced her; after all, I really did like her. But I just stood there stiffly, and my voice was flat and dry. Did I blame her? No—but I just couldn't hug her or kiss her or say to her, "I'm glad it worked out for you." I couldn't move. My hands were clenched, my heart was cold.

"I understand completely," I kept saying in that same odd, dry voice. "But you have to understand, too. I don't know what we'll do. I don't know if we'll manage to escape."

"You have to escape," Stefa repeated mechanically. She was already on the other side.

"Do you think"—I tried again—"that Paraska could persuade him?"

"No," Stefa replied. "It was difficult enough to persuade him to take me."

*

We were no longer a united group. Stefa and Paraska sat off by themselves, and, stunned and helpless, the four of us sat apart from them.

We had already decided: we would try to escape that night, as soon as the night shift set off. We knew this was wishful thinking. It seemed practically impossible that Schmidt wouldn't lock the door.

The commandant came in, yelling. His voice was loud and harsh, his angry face frightened us.

"Eat faster! *Schnell! Schnell!*" he shouted. "Night shift, get ready for work!"

Paraska was working the night shift. Suddenly I understood what Schmidt had meant when he said, "There's still time. I'll let you know." He had been waiting for Paraska's turn to work the night shift. She was the only one he was willing to help escape—and Stefa along with her. No one else. Had Paraska known this?

She stood beside her bunk, ready to go. She was round as a ball; she had on several layers of clothing. Stefa was also fatter than usual. She had tied a red scarf around her neck. She looked at us nervously. The night shift was assembling near the door. In a moment they would leave.

Elzbieta got up first, and I followed. Impulsively she

hugged Stefa and said, "I'm happy it worked out for you two."

I said, "Stay well."

Paraska urged her, "Hurry up. Don't make a scene." We kissed Stefa. She had tears in her eyes. At the last moment Zosia and Marysia came over. They said, "Farewell."

"Get moving! *Los!*" shouted Schmidt, and Paraska ran off with a few impatient backward glances at Stefa.

We lay on our bunks waiting for the night shift to leave the room. Then we calmly walked to the door.

It was locked.

*

We were trapped. The door was bolted. The windows were covered with wooden planks, nailed shut. In a few minutes the men in the factory would discover Paraska's absence. They would come here looking for her. Then they would discover Stefa's absence. In an hour or two they would come looking for us.

And so everything would be over. No one would ever know when or how. Suddenly I felt extremely curious. What would it feel like? How would I behave? I drank some water from the tap to calm myself, then I ate my ration of bread and margarine. Whenever things got very tense I had to eat or smoke. There were no cigarette butts left.

Calm down, be rational—no panic, no melodrama. If they didn't take us away during the night, we would escape in the morning on the way to work. We would get dressed as usual, so as not to provoke suspicion. As soon as we left the camp we'd veer left, slip through the gap in the wall and then, shielded by the wall, we would run away.

At the sound of the key in the lock, Elzbieta clutched my hand. But it was only Gandhi, who was on duty that night.

"Why hasn't Paraska gone to work?" he yelled.

"She has, she has. We saw her leave," said a few of the girls.

"But she's not in the factory!"

Paraska's bunk was empty, and so was Stefa's. The gray camp blankets were neatly folded.

"And the tall dark one? Where is Tarkowska?"

"Stefa went too," one of the girls remembered suddenly. "Stefa went to the factory."

"What? Where did she go? She works in the office. Why would she go to the factory at night? Where is the dark one?"

He rushed around the room, searching between the bunks. He even checked the toilet, then left, cursing loudly. He was afraid of Schmidt. If he only knew . . .

"Did they escape?" the girls were asking.

They were all looking at us. We didn't know anything, they had gone to the factory; Stefa, too—there was something she had to type.

But Gandhi was back already, bringing with him one of the girls from the night shift. He ordered someone to translate what she said. On the way to the plant, she'd seen Stefa and Paraska turn toward the river where, on the road to the camp of the Russian girls, a car was waiting. They had headed toward the car . . .

"They escaped!" Gandhi shook with rage. "They escaped! The two Jews escaped! Where are they? And the other ones?" He seemed suddenly to have remembered us.

He didn't have to look very hard. We were all sitting in a row on one of the bunks.

After he left, there was an uproar.

"Is it really true?"

"How lucky! They succeeded."

"Who knows? They might get caught."

"Strange that Schmidt didn't notice!"

"Oh, he was close to Paraska."

"So what? That doesn't mean he'd let her escape."

"They didn't tell you anything? No?"

"And you're not running away?"

"Run away, girls. You really should."

"How are they supposed to run away if the door is locked?"

"There'll be time tomorrow."

"Oh, come on, tomorrow they'll be taken away."

"Maybe not. They said Thursday, and tomorrow is only Wednesday."

"Run away. We won't tell."

"No," we said. "We're not running away." We denied it, because we were afraid to tell the truth, even though the girls in the room were now genuinely moved—as if a shock had restored them to their senses, as if they suddenly understood. For the first time they were acting the way they should have acted all along.

But the last few months had wiped out the last vestiges of trust in us. Telling them not to breathe a word, we confided in a few girls: we were planning to escape the next evening. Several minutes later, everyone in the room was whispering, "May God keep them from being taken away before that. It would be a great pity."

Only Anielka didn't believe us, and we told her the truth. She wanted to escape with us. We couldn't understand it.

"Perhaps you're also a 'city' girl?" we asked, forgetting that she didn't know our code. "I am from the city," she answered, surprised. "I come from Lvov. But what difference does that make?"

No. She was not Jewish. She had had enough of the camp, but would never have decided to escape on her own. Besides, she had grown attached to us. Did she realize the risks? we asked. Yes, only it was not so dangerous for her as it was for us, because she really was a Pole. And Michasia was escaping, too, she pointed out, even though her name wasn't on the list. We couldn't dissuade her.

Nighttime. Stefa and Paraska were already far from town. Where were they going? With whom were they riding in that small car that waited near the river?

I lay on my back covered with my coat. I lay stiff and motionless, afraid to move, afraid to open my eyes. It felt good. I wouldn't think anymore or make any more plans. It wasn't worth it. Let everything take its course. All the young people in our family had perished. Maybe it was predestined, maybe it was a sign that we, too . . .

This thought made me sit bolt upright on my bunk.

No. I can't think like that. There's no such thing as destiny.
We had succeeded so many times, tomorrow morning, in
the darkness, no one would see us, one leap through
the gap in the wall, and then straight ahead, straight
ahead . . . We would succeed, we had to succeed, we had
always succeeded, and then to the forest, and in the evening
to the train station, and from there, on the train . . .

"Katarzyna, you're not asleep, are you?" Helena Pajaczkowska asked from the upper bunk.

Since the night she came back drunk, we hadn't
spoken a single word.

"Katarzyna, dear, I just wanted to ask you a question."

I was silent.

"I just wanted to ask whether . . . if something happens
to you . . . if they . . . can I take your things? Would that
be all right?"

I covered my ears with my hands.

Two in the morning. Perhaps they wouldn't come. I
fell asleep. I was dreaming about a garden. Marian's voice
was calling my name. "That's not my name," I said, and
woke up. My heart was pounding. I sat up. In the bunk
above mine, Helena's head popped up.

"Katarzyna, don't forget to leave the key to your
suitcase."

*

We washed at the tap, polished our shoes, drank our
coffee, just like every day. My mind was blank. Gandhi
stood at the door and didn't take his eyes off us. The crowd
near the door was growing. Then, just like every day:

"Ready? Let's go! *Los!*" I gripped Elzbieta's hand. One more minute, two. I turned around and saw Zosia's huge blue eyes, and Marysia's blue coat.

"Majewska, come over here!"

Gandhi's hands moved over my body, searching through my pockets. There was nothing in them except a dirty handkerchief. It was very quiet in the room. The girls watched in astonishment as Gandhi frisked Zosia, Elzbieta, and Marysia. Finally a wave of cold air rushed into the room. Outside the door was total darkness.

I squeezed Elzbieta's hand hard. A gust of wind carried us forward. We were running, gasping for breath. Elzbieta was limping, it was hard for her to run. Hurry, hurry, somebody's footsteps right behind us, someone was following us, faster, faster . . . I was out of breath, I staggered, I leaned against something hard. A fence, an ordinary wooden fence. Behind Marysia, Michasia and Anielka were running. Zosia was not with them. We waited to see if she was coming, we listened for her footsteps, but there was nothing, only silence and darkness.

We were running again, without knowing where we were running, except that it was away from the camp. The muddy alley turned into a paved road. We slowed down. The streets were still empty; the town was waking up.

Elzbieta, Michasia, and Anielka crossed the road. We walked parallel to each other, on opposite sides of the street.

From around the corner a man's figure appeared: an officer's cap, high boots, a springy walk. Even before he approached us, we knew who it was.

We stood there staring at each other. On the other side of the street, the other three had also stopped.

Schmidt asked: "Where are you going?"

"We're running away" I answered.

"So you're running away . . ." he repeated and slowly removed his hand from his pocket. I had seen that gesture before. I thought: He's going to shoot us. He raised his arm to look at his wristwatch.

"The train leaves at seven. You can still make it. Take the train. Don't waste time."

He took a piece of paper out of his wallet, scribbled a few words on it, and handed it to Marysia.

"This is my address. Write to me."

We were speechless with amazement.

"You're a brave bunch . . . a brave bunch . . ."

He turned and walked away.

"*Elsbeth!*" I shouted in German. I hadn't seen her standing right beside me. "Where are the others?"

"They got scared, they turned back."

At that instant, without thinking, we started running toward the center of town.

We ran into the town, which was still dark. All we knew was that the train station was somewhere in the center . . . I can't remember anything about that first short distance we ran, shaken and stunned by our meeting with Schmidt, and by what he said to us, I can't see those running people, I can't hear their footsteps. But the image of train tracks unexpectedly cutting across the street is as clear as a photograph: the street narrows, and the tracks cut across it, diagonally, then disappear toward the right between the high walls of the tunnel, the open tunnel without a ceiling. Without a word, with only one thought, we began to run along the tracks. And from then on, despite the darkness, I can see everything. Hidden by the walls, we kept on running, tripping over the railroad ties, the gravel crunching and sliding from under our feet. I can hear our harsh panting. Ahead of us a lantern shone in the distance. Someone shouted, "Joseph, is that you?" and repeated it once or twice while we clung fast to the rough stone wall, glued there by sticky, cold fear. For one long moment the lantern hung motionless in the air, and then darkness again surrounded us. I don't know how long we ran.

Suddenly the tunnel grew brighter as it opened onto the station plaza and the gray dawn light.

We watched from our hiding place as a column of young women walked toward the station. We recognized them by the gray kerchiefs tied tightly around their heads: they were Russians. They might have been the Russians from our factory—rumor had it that they would soon be transferred to a different city—but they also might have been Russians from a different camp. There were more camps than factories in that city.

The column of girls circled the station building and disappeared. Soon after, a car arrived, and a young woman in a light fur coat stepped out followed by a military officer. I felt a sudden pang of fear: they were looking for us, they'd be waiting for us.

The clock above the station entrance said six-forty. It was time. Silently, we tied our scarves into turbans. That was how the German women in the factory wore them, and we had to make ourselves look as German as possible: neat and cared for, every hair in its place, every button buttoned, calm, and a little dull-witted.

Marysia's cheeks were burning; mine were, too. Elzbieta's were pale and bloodless.

No one was waiting for us. The small station lobby was filled with commuters taking the seven-o'clock train to work. The men's flat caps reminded me of Gandhi and his shrill voice, "You won't get away . . ." A few people looked

at me as if to say: I haven't seen *you* here before. I searched
for the woman in the fur coat and the military man. They
stood in a niche, encircled by a plume of cigarette smoke,
staring into one another's eyes.

"*Dreimal bitte, dritte Klasse* . . ." My voice was slightly
higher than normal. As I counted the money, my fingers
shook a little. It was almost seven. Klautz had already arrived
in the office to pick up the measurements from the last few
days. "Don't be insolent, you . . . you . . ." He had never
said the word, but he would certainly be saying it today.
Everybody would be saying, "Those were Jews who ran
away."

Please, let the train come . . .

It was a commuter train, which meant it would be a
short trip. "I'll go alone," whispered Marysia, "Let's meet
by the exit." That was sensible; it would be safer. But I
knew that she was afraid of Elzbieta's black hair, that she
was fleeing from it, and that she had had this fear all
along.

Elzbieta and I entered a smoky compartment. I immediately longed for a cigarette. One seat was still empty.
Elzbieta sat down, closed her eyes and pretended to be
asleep. I stood by the window. Between the narrow streams
of water trickling down the pane, I could see the last two
letters of the name of the station: "——RG." Then a pale,
milky fog clouded the window, the letters vanished, and it
was as if a pale, milky curtain covered the months in the
camp, the room with bunk beds, the girls and Schmidt.

I bent my knees a little, swaying with the train as it
gathered speed. I felt as if I were climbing higher and

higher. Joy filled my heart. I breathed deeply and freely, a brief moment of euphoria which subsided almost immediately and left a painful, empty hollowness. I reminded myself: Don't be happy. We'd taken the first—the hardest—step, but it didn't mean a thing. We would arrive, get off, and then what? Where would we go then?

Elzbieta opened her eyes. We exchanged quick, shy smiles.

The town was small and empty. We walked briskly down the main street, singing *"Everything passes; night turns to day."* We carried that popular tune like a banner: Look, here are three cheerful German girls, happy with themselves and with life. *"After December, always comes May,"* they sang, walking briskly, like people with somewhere to go.

It was hard to tell for whom we were singing, because the street was deserted. Perhaps we were singing for ourselves, singing that this, too, would pass. Only when we were outside the town did we fall silent, and the smiles faded from our lips.

We turned into a nearby forest. It was a young forest, with small, thin, naked trees, but compared to the open road it felt sheltered and safe. We decided to stay there until evening and only move on after dark. In silence, we lay down on a pile of dry leaves. There were so many things we had to discuss, so many questions we had to answer. We lay there, suddenly faint, exhausted and intoxicated by the fresh air. Delicate as spider webs, clouds floated across the pale, bleached sky. The sun was hidden and yet, looking up, we had to squint. Below us, in a little hollow, was a narrow, well-trodden footpath; we could hear a dog barking, far away.

We slept for a long time. The sun was now directly overhead: white, wintery, and cold. Without getting up from the pile of leaves, we talked about Schmidt, the same question, over and over—what kind of person was he really? We couldn't be sure. At first, he seemed friendly—*seemed*, because it wasn't clear if that wasn't just his tricky way of making the others envy us. Or was he genuinely friendly? And then he seemed so hostile. And yet he helped us. He had helped Paraska because he slept with her. *Rassenschande*, miscegenation—he could be severely punished for disgracing the race. Had Paraska realized that? But in the end he let us walk away, too. He did what he was supposed to do, he notified the Gestapo—and then he helped us. He hadn't meant to help us—it was a coincidence that he ran into us—but he didn't stop us, and he could have. He said that the train was leaving at seven and told us to write to him. He gave us his address. So? It was impossible to tell . . . or perhaps . . .

But enough of this conversation which led nowhere. We would not solve anything, here and now, on a pile of dead leaves. Perhaps after the war—that is, if we survived; we never forgot to add those words. After the war, if we survived, I also wanted to ask Helena about that night when she came back drunk and cried on my bunk. Did she voluntarily sign the denunciation? Or did Schmidt—whom she'd already told about us—insist she sign, and she then consented eagerly, thinking about the reward she'd been promised, the job of switchboard operator. I really wanted to ask her. Of course, I couldn't have known that neither Helena nor Schmidt would survive the war, that they would die during an air raid.

"Shall we write to him?" asked Marysia.

"No, we can't. After the war, if . . ."

"But I have to write to Paulina. I have to ask her not to send packages through that German friend of hers. It could be risky for her. Besides, I don't want to lose contact with her. I will write to Paulina," she repeated, and waited to hear what we would say. We were silent. We didn't say, "Don't write, it's dangerous." We knew she would write to Paulina anyway.

The only things we didn't discuss were the things that mattered most. Those we circled around, avoided, pushed away. Cold as it was, the sun warmed us; sleepiness overcame us again. Our eyelids closed, as if of their own volition. We were only an hour by train from the camp. They were looking for us. Meanwhile, in the forest, we were lying on the ground, fast asleep.

*

Katarzyna, Elzbieta, and Marysia stayed behind on that pile of leaves. Katarzyna's place was taken by Joanna Pilecka, Elzbieta's by Jadwiga Kotula. They were our school friends, and we knew they had been taken to work in Germany. Marysia assumed the name of Anna Kloc. These new names were not corroborated by any documents, and the lack of documents required some explanation.

Joanna, Jadwiga, and Anna: three simple country girls

who had escaped from a transport when their train stopped at a station in a German town whose name they didn't know. They escaped, and immediately, at the same train station, were captured and returned to the train. They threatened to escape again, they wanted to go home, to Poland. To prevent them from running away, their documents were taken. They didn't care. They escaped at the next stop, without documents.

*

We left the forest at twilight and returned to the train station: it was dark and empty. The next train was leaving for Hagen. It would have been better to get far away in one big jump—Munich . . . Vienna . . . But that was impossible. In order to buy tickets for longer trips, passengers had to show identification. So we had to travel in short segments.

This time the three of us boarded the same car. Anna didn't want to be separated from us anymore.

A young woman in mourning clothes sat alone in a long, open car. We took the seats furthest away from her. I didn't look at the German woman but at the dark window; still, I could see the reflection of her face, turned toward us. I could also see the elaborate turbans on our heads. The light was faint, yellowish, just as it had been in the train where I'd seen, reflected in the window pane, the kidskin gloves of the young informer. I didn't like the way the woman kept looking at us, even though, unlike the informer, she saw us only as young foreigners, brought here to work, now traveling illegally, without passes; perhaps we had escaped from a factory or a farm. I didn't like her suspicious gaze.

As she handed the conductor her ticket, she motioned toward us with her head. The train was slowing down, pulling into a station. The conductor said, "I'll be right back," and left.

We, too, left, quickly, out the other door. The station was small, the platform empty. We ran down the stairs. The ticket collector at the door was surprised by our haste. Probably he would have been even more amazed if he'd realized that all three of us were interrupting a trip we'd just begun, getting off at the first stop. But he would never know.

Suddenly a siren wailed deafeningly. People were running, and we ran, too. They were rushing to their air-raid shelters, we were running out of town, running down a highway past heaps of black coal, black chimneys, toward a huge bridge.

We ran down a steep slope and across a muddy field. Suddenly we smelled a river—was it still the brackish, brown Ruhr? We sat down and leaned against the pillars supporting the bridge's enormous spans. Above us, markers burst into the night like bright Christmas trees, cones of light swept the sky. We heard the drone of bombers. We sat curled up, our heads between our hunched shoulders. The ground beneath us shook.

When it got quiet and dark, we climbed back up to the highway and walked straight ahead.

We would travel at night and sleep in the forest during

the day. We would walk as far as possible from the camp, we would walk as long as we had the strength.

*

In vain we tried to find our way out of the forest, which was probably quite ordinary, neither huge nor impenetrable. But night seemed to enlarge its dimensions; the darkness made its depths seem deeper. The branches groaned in the wind, and the light, constant rustle of leaves sounded like a swollen stream.

We had lost our way and were pushing through the thick underbrush; our hands tore at the branches, untangling their knots. Every few minutes we stopped to listen for sounds other than those of the forest, the sound of a passing car, for example, or a barking dog. But there was nothing. The sky above us was dark and moonless, and the wind was strangely warm, even though it was winter.

Suddenly the forest rose higher. We were walking uphill when we should have been walking down. Our climbing was futile. And suddenly everything seemed as futile as our efforts to get back to the highway.

Walking up ahead of us, Anna screamed, sank to the ground, and began to cry. We had come full circle back to the place we had left at twilight. The grass was still flattened from our having lain there all day, and a tall tree stump, cut straight across, was impossible to mistake.

I was sharply aware of how quickly the night was passing, how few hours remained, how we needed to make progress—and not wander about aimlessly. I closed my eyes and tried to remember how we'd entered this little glade at dawn; how, pushing aside the wet hazel branches, we'd first seen the circular clearing and in its center a tree stump, slightly taller than the rest. I recalled a moment from the day before, when we'd pushed aside some other hazel branches and entered a clearing, similar but different, without the cut trees and without that tall stump. That was our first stop in the forest, after the first night of walking, but now I needed to recall the second stop and the second day. I had been walking in front, Jadwiga behind me, Anna behind Jadwiga. "We can stay here," I had said, and now, without opening my eyes, I whispered the same words.

"We can stay here," I had said then and bent down because something crumpled under my feet in the grass—an empty Sulima cigarette pack. I had picked it up and dropped it again. Calling up all these details exhausted me, but now I knew what we had do.

I searched the clearing for the Sulima box. It lay on a clump of moss. I pushed the branches aside: there was no footpath, and this seemed right. Because now I remembered that the path ended lower down, at a place where a broken, dead branch hung from a tree, a branch that we had mistaken for the silhouette of a thin man.

We walked down slowly, peering into the darkness for the telling details we had noticed that morning: a tin can on the path, a bunch of straw, huge stands of ferns, neat stacks of wood, ready to be taken away.

We had to wait before we could get back on the highway. A convoy of trucks was passing by. We lay in a drainage ditch. The warmth of our bodies melted the snow, and I could feel the moisture seeping through my coat. The ditch was deep enough to lie in, and because of the soft snow that remained, almost as comfortable as a bed.

When the silence returned, and darkness again shrouded the highway, we started walking in the formation that had become our habit: one behind the other, along the edge of the pavement, near the ditch, our only protection. Only Jadwiga's limping disturbed the even rhythm of our march.

I tried to concentrate on walking and not think about anything—not think back, or ahead. But I kept feeling that this was all a dream, that someone was about to wake me with a shout—*Aufstehen!*—that I was dozing on my bunk. I was trying to stay alert, but I kept drifting off.

"We're walking in circles," Anna said again and again. I stopped paying attention to her.

A road sign stood at an intersection, like a motionless windmill with its arms spread wide. We could hardly read the writing. The names told us nothing. We had never heard of them. So, just as we had the night before, we chose the town with the nicest-sounding name. That was easy enough, since all but one sounded harsh, full of short syllables clumsily joined together. But that one sounded nice. It made us think of meadows, and hinted at rewards.

So we went toward the city—or was it a town?—named Iserlohn. There was a lot of traffic that night, and we kept having to lie down in the ditch. Our clothes, our stockings, and our shoes were wet. It was harder and harder to keep marching. Jadwiga fell behind because of her injured foot. Our pace slowed drastically—not because of

Jadwiga's foot, but because it was our second night of marching and our second day without food.

Probably that was when, dazed by exhaustion, we strayed from the highway. We were surprised by the sudden softness beneath our feet. The pavement had stopped, and the soft earth was soothing, lulling. The headlights of a passing car glittered in the distance. We turned quickly back toward the road, but in vain; the highway had disappeared as if it had never existed, and all at once we were walking between dark silent houses, down a narrow winding village lane.

At first we were afraid that our footsteps would wake the dogs, who would start barking. Then we would be trapped. But not a sound broke the silence, and then it was the silence itself that we feared. With our arms stretched out in front of us, we wandered between the houses, trying to get clear of them, out into the open. But we were completely surrounded: houses and walls, fences and ladders, benches, trees and wells. We walked gingerly, on tiptoe, trying not to wake the people sleeping in their feather-beds—or the dogs in their doghouses. There was not a sound to be heard in this mute, silent village.

"Doesn't it seem strange to you?" whispered Anna. "Not even a barking dog. No one lives here. This village is dead." And then I no longer saw the people in their featherbeds or the dogs in their doghouses, but, rather, rooms stripped of furniture, bare walls, and a silence uninterrupted even by the quiet sound of breathing.

Angrily, I said, "That's nonsense." But deep in my heart, I agreed with Anna. This was no ordinary village.

"They took them away, they've been evacuated," she kept whispering intensely. "There must be a camp nearby."

"Have you gone mad?" I wanted to yell. But I didn't yell.

I looked at the sky, searching for the first signs of dawn. The sky was dark, covered with thick clouds, without a single star. I didn't even notice that we had broken out of the labyrinth of buildings, and were now walking on a muddy path through an open field. I heard Anna cry out. Painfully, despite my exhaustion, I ran toward her, with Jadwiga behind me.

"Touch it," said Anna, and there was a note of triumph in her voice. "Just as I said: wire."

With that, she sat down on the ground. Jadwiga sat, too. I reached out my arm. The wire was cold, smooth, moist.

For a while I tried to collect my thoughts, to remember something very important, but my thoughts were too scattered, and I couldn't collect them. I felt myself slowly slumping to the ground. "In just a moment, in a moment I'll remember it," I thought. It was the last thing I thought before I fell asleep.

We were awakened by roosters crowing. We were lying on a footpath under the wire fence of a pasture, near a small, tidy village. Curtains hung in the windows, flowers bloomed in pots. In the meadow stood a well with a watering trough. Only grazing cows were missing; they were still in their sheds for the winter.

We got up quickly, looking for a forest. There was one nearby, just past the meadow—a dense, old growth.

We crept through the bushes near the edge of the forest.

I suddenly remembered: "How could you?" I asked Anna. "That was just plain pasture wire, completely smooth."

We went back to sleep.

*

Every so often, hunger woke us with intense hollow pangs, and then we would sink back into a restless sleep. That was a bad day, the day that preceded our third night of marching. The memory of the dead village was also bad. I was troubled by how easily I had succumbed to Anna's hallucinations, her vision of the empty houses and the camp. Hunger and hallucination. We had to keep our wits.

We would only be able to stand one more night of marching at the most, I thought, and a moment later I heard the slapping sound of Agafia's slippers. "Your young man has arrived," she was saying, and I ran to the porch; Marian stood there, oddly dressed, in an elegant fur coat, high boots, a hat with a shiny feather. He said, "I came to say goodbye, or to stay."

I woke up moaning. The emptiness in my stomach felt as heavy as a stone. When I opened my eyes, I saw Jadwiga and Anna under the bushes, I saw their pale faces, and I could see myself, as if from above, as if I had split into two people—one lying there, and the other one watching her.

Exhausting naps, hallucinatory dreams. I knew we should knock on a peasant's door as soon as possible and say "*Pole*" and "*Arbeit*." In the camp they used to say that if you found a German who needed a worker, he might take care of all the formalities himself at the *Arbeitsamt*, without involving the police. But when dusk came we all agreed to march on for a third night; out of cowardice, we postponed the critical moment of knocking on someone's door, the moment that could bring good fortune as well as very bad.

We trudged forward wearily. Right at the beginning of that march Jadwiga imagined a huge, white house. It blocked her way and forced her to veer to the center of the highway. Later, she saw other huge houses, all of them white and beautiful. She described them in detail. Ignoring her resistance and her complaints, we took her by the arm and led her back to the edge of the highway, near the ditch. When her mind cleared, she said, "I'm hallucinating."

We sat down on a rise behind a cluster of trees. In front of us was a village we had no way of avoiding. In the distance, to the right, the lights of some town flickered tentatively. Jadwiga put some snow on her eyes, to make the buildings disappear. A motorcycle roared past on the highway, then another and another.

"That's the search party," said Anna. "They're after us. Look!"

I looked at the distant, yellow lights. They flickered like a candle flame and suddenly began to move. They were speeding toward us. Once more we heard the sound of an engine, and Anna said, "They're after us. It's the search party."

The lights zoomed toward us, then receded back to where they had been, and a moment later began their crazy trip again. I felt dizzy. I lay on the ground and closed my eyes. Now I was hallucinating. We have to do it right away, I thought, we have to knock on someone's door, here, in this village . . .

A two-story cottage stood alone on a small hill. Light shone through its drawn curtains. It was not late. Jadwiga sat down on a little bench near the entrance. Anna and I went up to the door. "Remember, we don't know German," I said to Anna, and knocked.

We heard footsteps. A woman's voice asked, "Who's there?" We didn't answer. "Who's there?" the woman repeated, loudly, impatiently. The door opened slightly. An old woman with gray hair regarded us with astonishment.

"*Arbeit. Pole*," we both said at once.

She immediately opened the door wider, pulled us inside, and turned the key in the lock.

The room was large, dimly lit, sparsely furnished. Wooden stairs led to a second floor.

The woman cried out, "Walter! Come here, *schnell!*"

A heavy young German man in an unbuttoned shirt ran down the stairs.

"Who are these girls, mother?"

"They only said '*Arbeit*' and '*Pole*.' I think that we should . . ."

He came closer. He had slightly bulging eyes and an unhealthy complexion.

"Where did you escape from? Which factory?"

"*Nix* factory."

"Papers!"

"*Nix.*"

He whistled through his teeth.

"I'll call the police." He turned to his mother. "I'll tell them to come to the tavern. Meanwhile, you keep an eye on them."

The German woman asked if we'd eaten, and a moment later brought two slices of bread spread with beet marmalade.

"Wir—drei." I held up three fingers.

"*Du lieber Gott!* Where's the third one?"

I went out to get her. Jadwiga got up from the bench. She said, "What did they . . . ?"

I said, "Come in. You'll get some bread with marmalade."

"But what about . . . ?"

"Her son is calling the authorities. I deliberately avoided the word "police." I didn't want to let them know that I understood their German.

We could hardly chew the bread, our jaws were so rusty.

Walter came back dressed in a green hunting jacket. He froze when he saw Jadwiga.

"What's this? Another one? Good God! How many are there?"

The moment we walked into the tavern, I knew why he had brought us there. In the kitchen, near the sink, stood a young woman in wooden clogs. A suntanned young man was drinking coffee at the table. They were Polish.

"You will translate," the German told the young man.

"The police will be coming shortly. They are Polish. We don't know where they escaped from. They don't speak a word of German."

"Are you Polish?" I asked the young man excitedly. "That's wonderful. We can't communicate with them. Please tell him we escaped from the train."

"A policeman's on the way. Then I'll tell him," he said grudgingly. Without interrupting her work, the girl said, "Why did you run away? When they catch you, they beat you."

Two policemen appeared at the door. The boy translated our story about the escape from the train. The older policeman, who had a mustache, took notes.

The girl repeated, "Why'd you go to all the trouble? You couldn't make it to Poland. It's too far."

We were led down a country road, lined on both sides by trees. The calm. Soft lights in the windows. Sudden relief.

*

That night we slept in a prison cell, all of us in one bunk. The wall above the bunk was covered with graffiti: *Just until spring. Vive la liberté. Let's kick the Krauts' asses. Long live Poland.* Polish names, French names, Russian names . . . mostly Polish. We told each other that all the people who had left their marks on the wall were people who had been brought to Germany, escapees from labor camps, like us. We told each other that our case was not so unusual, though we knew that this wasn't true and that any similarity was an illusion. But saying so gave us hope.

The Journey

I was awakened by a dream. An SS man was standing over my mother's sickbed. The room was empty, it had been looted. I could see his face clearly. I watched him— as I had then—from the corner of the room where he had ordered us to stand without moving. It took all my strength to chase that image from my mind. I looked at the barred window. Dawn was breaking.

But I can't remember the police interrogation that took place that morning with the aid of an official interpreter. Why has the interpreter vanished from my mind: his questions, our answers, our trip to the city on the train? All that remains of that scene is one sentence spoken by the policeman with the mustache. "Take them to Iserlohn, to the *Arbeitsamt.*"

To Iserlohn! The city we had chosen at the crossroads during the night because we were attracted by its name, so different from the other, harsh names. I can't remember the city, either. I know the policeman led us through the streets from the train station to the *Arbeitsamt* . . . I know it, but I can't remember.

*

A stocky German, his face deformed by a protruding eye, sat behind the desk in the *Arbeitsamt*. He already knew about us—"So these are the three." The Cyclops eye rested on us with menace, suspicion, contempt. I felt a stupid smile spread across my face; I hadn't used that grin for a while, but it was always there, ready. The official dismissed the policeman and carefully read the report. When he finished, he yanked his desk drawer open and took from it a rubber truncheon that he placed before him on the desk.

"No lies!" he shouted. "No tricks! Otherwise . . . Understand?"

We shook our heads. *"Nix, nix."*

"Translation!"

A small, stooped man in a frayed suit hurried into the room and said to us in broken Polish:

"I can talk a little Polish, and I will be translating what you will say, and you will tell truth because otherwise you'll be in big trouble. Where from run away?"

I stared at him as if I were staring at a rainbow. "Oh, Sir, the Lord must have sent you from heaven! Please help us! Why is that man yelling at us? It's all written down right there: we ran away from the train." There were tears in my voice.

"What was the name of the station? Who took their documents away?" barked the Cyclops. He didn't believe us.

"We don't know what the name of that station was. Some kind of German name, and we can't understand their talk. It was huge. The train stood there for a long time. Where were we escaping to? Oh, sir, where else would we go but back home to Poland? Please tell him that we want to go home."

"To Poland?" The German was getting angrier. "Rubbish! On foot, without money, without documents? They're not that dumb." A vein in his forehead was pulsing.

"How did you know the way?" asked the interpreter.

"We were following the sun, sir, following the good sun in heaven."

My voice stopped, hung in midair. I began to cry—real tears. The interpreter said, "There, there, be quiet. Enough. I will tell him. Be quiet. Enough. Enough."

I wiped my eyes with the back of my hand.

"You're Polish yourself. You understand that we . . ."

Oh, how easy it was to cry, what a pleasure! I was a stupid, simple girl, running away to Poland, following the good sun in God's heaven. "Bravo," I told myself, "you're doing fine, but be careful, don't push it."

Weeping, I said, "They were taking us to a factory, sir. At home we'd never laid eyes on a factory. We worked in the fields, on a farm. We're no good with machines."

"You're so stupid! You can't walk to Poland, not even if you walk for a month. And there's the same work here, in the fields."

"So please tell him we're used to farm work, that he should send us to a village."

"Can you milk?"

"And how!"

For a long time they whispered together. Finally the official raised his arms, grabbed an imaginary cow's udder, pulled it a few times, and ordered the interpreter to ask us how many cows each of us had had at home.

I wiped my eyes again.

Jadwiga had had three cows, Anna two. I had a goat.

They decided to send us to three different places. This would prevent any possibility of escape, which, the Cyclops warned us, would certainly lead to our being sent to a concentration camp. After he'd announced that, he ordered us out and told us to wait in the hallway.

Anna left first. The farmer who came to pick her up looked more like an estate owner than a peasant. He wore a green jacket with braided trim, a hunting hat, and boots polished to a high gloss. They left in a car.

Jadwiga and I left on a train, with a clerk from the *Arbeitsamt* whose hair was as red as a squirrel's.

We were being separated for the first time. At a little train station, a buggy with two horses was waiting, and an old man with a long, white beard sat in the coachman's seat. All around us were meadows and forests. Jadwiga's face looked as painfully drawn as it had at Halinka's. And I said to her, just as I had at Halinka's, "Don't start bawling," though Jadwiga wasn't crying this time, either. I also said, "I'll come see you."

She got into the little carriage. She was so skinny—only now did I notice how much weight she had lost. She turned around, once, twice. The old man said something to her. She shook her head, probably to let him know that she didn't understand. The buggy left. The train took off. I stared out the window at the landscape cloaked in mist.

We got off at a small, busy station. Huge posters counseled alertness: PSST! THE ENEMY HAS EARS! Next to the poster stood a tall, middle-aged man, with a long, narrow face, like a wolf's: a dark face, with tiny black eyes.

"This is the Polish girl, Joanna," said the clerk. "And this is your boss, Herr Schulz."

I smiled. Joanna would be different from Katarzyna. She would be cheerful, optimistic, naïve—but not stupid.

"Can you milk?" asked Schulz. Like Anna's farmer, he wore green hunter's clothes and didn't look like a peasant.

"She doesn't understand a word," explained the red-haired clerk.

"That doesn't matter. We have two Poles at our place. They'll teach her. The most important thing is that she knows how to milk. "*Joanna, kannst du . . . so?* He pumped his arms in the air. I had to stop myself from laughing.

"Yes, yes, she milks fine," the clerk assured him, praising his merchandise. He shook his finger at me and warned me not to run away—"*Nix weglaufen!*"—and then left.

To my surprise, Waldwiesen turned out to be a little town, not a village. Red brick houses lined the streets, and one of them belonged to my "boss," Wilhelm Schulz. His house had three stories and was narrow and deep; the back of the house extended into the yard in which there was a huge barn with a gate painted light blue, the color of sea-water. (Later, I often looked at this gate from the window of my room upstairs; its color soothed me.) The barn and the huge square barnyard convinced me that this was a farm, after all. Schulz pushed open a low door—it was not the main entrance—and we entered a dark, tidy kitchen. At a round table sat a middle-aged woman. Her skin was very white. She had smooth brown hair. Her face was pretty but charmless, cold.

"Here we are," said Schulz. "Her name is Joanna. She can't speak German. She has no possessions, nothing."

As she listened, Klothilde Schulz ladled some split-pea soup with bacon into a bowl and said, "Eat this. Afterwards you will clean the windows. Today is Saturday. On Saturday the windows are cleaned." Her voice was high-pitched, sharp; her movements were brisk. She opened a side door. Just outside it, amazingly, the face of a cow looked in at me. She shouted, "Jan!"

A moment later a hunchbacked young man entered the kitchen. We shook hands.

"The old lady says you should eat the soup and then clean the windows. There's a hell of a lot of work in this place. We'll tell you everything, a little at a time. Or, rather, Walenty will tell you—he's smarter than me. Can you milk? Because ever since the Serbian girl left, I've had to do all the goddamn milking myself."

I gulped down the soup. Bacon, which I used to hate, tasted delicious. Klothilde disappeared for a moment and returned with an old plaid dress with patches on the elbows. At first, I almost recoiled, but luckily I managed to control that impulse. I would mend this dress and save the clothes I was wearing now, in case of another escape.

She gave herself a month to wait. After a month she decided to stop waiting, stop worrying about the arrival of the police, stop fearing she'd be found out.

This was her principal fear, but it wasn't her only one. There were also other fears, about things that seemed less important, but were potentially just as dangerous. For example, she worried that her unfamiliarity with the customs of the farm and her inability to perform various chores would arouse suspicion and betray the fact that she wasn't the person she was pretending to be. She carefully hid the blisters she got on her hands from digging with a shovel; she became an expert at ignoring pain. But she could not hide her inability to milk cows, feed pigs, or clean windows. This last was exposed on the very first day: the longer she cleaned the glass, the cloudier it became. All she could do was try to hide her deficiencies, employ all sorts of tricks to distract the others' attention, and acquire the new skills as soon as she could.

She became shrewd and calculating. She observed, imitated, hid, protected herself with laughter and jokes. The cows stopped kicking and angrily switching their tails. After a week, she was milking five cows, three times a day. Janek milked the other five. Walenty didn't take care of the cows, only the horses. Awakened each morning by Klothilde's horrible bell, she ran cheerfully downstairs to her work in the kitchen, the field, the garden, the pigsty, always singing the same three folk songs—the only songs she remembered. Janek giggled. He said, "That Joanna's such a cheerful girl." Walenty, who was reserved, smiled faintly. He was the only one who had noticed the blisters on her fingers: unexpectedly, he grabbed her hand and turned it over—and was shocked. "For the love of God, girl . . ." He gave her a piece of pork fat to rub on her sores. He didn't say a word to the farmers, but only joked that her hands were delicate, meant for the piano and not for a shovel.

Walenty, a peasant from Pomerania, was married, spoke fairly good German, and was Schulz's right-hand man. He made her a little nervous. He sat at the table— the three of them ate together—neatly attired, in contrast to (and clearly contemptuous of) the sloppy Janek. Walenty was well built, round-faced, and slightly balding. A white collar buttoned up under his chin gave him the look of a country priest. Close-mouthed and with a sarcastic smile, he was respected by the Poles but had no friends. People called him "a decent man," though they also said he was out for himself. His behavior toward the "bosses" was distant and discreet. She respected him for this, and acted the same way.

The master and the mistress belonged to a class known as *Grossbauern*: wealthy farmers, part peasant, part townspeople. One morning she came upon Klothilde in the cow shed with her skirt hiked up. Another time she saw her getting into a car, dressed up in a fur coat and a hat, amid a cloud of perfume; she was on her way to the theater.

Klothilde ran her household with an iron hand. There was a rule and a routine for everything. Every day of the week had its own invariable dish: they ate "spinach" (actually, nettles) every Tuesday, potato pancakes on Friday, meat on Sunday and holidays. In the basement, lined up on the shelves like books in a library, were jars of pickled pork. Every jar was numbered and marked with the date of the slaughter. Currently they were eating the year 1940.

Proudly, Klothilde gave her a tour of that kingdom of slaughtered pigs, fruit preserves, and marinated vegetables. Her pride was completely justified. The collection was impressive, but Joanna walked past it indifferently, refusing to admire it.

The month she'd set aside for waiting was about to end. The pain brought on by the long hours of field work disappeared; the blisters scabbed over. Quickly, but not too quickly, she was "learning" German. Her vocabulary grew. She was starting to put sentences together, though she always used the infinitive form of verbs, the way foreigners did.

She went to the police with Schulz and obtained an identification card with seals and with her fingerprints, officially confirming that she was Joanna Pilecka. For the first time she felt something like quiet satisfaction.

She became friends with Magda, who worked at the Count's. On Sundays she used to go with Walenty and Janek to the Count's estate a few miles outside town. Magda was a maid there, Jurek was a gardener. Poles often gathered there on Sundays.

Early spring was approaching. The grounds of the estate were turning green. The ponds were covered with young duckweed. Magda, who was tall and statuesque, had a little round room in a tower on the third floor of the castle. She proudly showed Joanna a china chamber pot hidden in the nightstand. She said, "See how well off I am?" In the morning, she poured the contents onto the tops of the tall trees. They both laughed. Joanna looked at the sweeping view, at the paths, trees, lanes, lawns, and flower beds, and beyond them, at the meadows, endless meadows through which flowed the wide, graceful river, still the same Ruhr.

"What are you looking at?" Magda would ask. "There's nothing there to look at."

One day, coming down the winding stairs of the tower, they ran into the Count. On leave from the army, he was wearing his uniform and had a monocle crooked in one of his blue eyes. The ghetto rose up before her.

The Count lifted her chin with one finger. He seemed surprised. "This one looks like a German."

In the gardener's cottage—where Jurek lived—she scrubbed her chin with water.

The first time she had come there, Jurek had praised Hitler for "taking care" of the Jews. A tall, suntanned young man sitting next to the window had exclaimed, "How can you say such a thing! Aren't you ashamed? You know what he . . . what's happened to the Jews."

"Listen to him!" Jurek laughed. "Maybe you're a Jew yourself?"

She had thought: Remember that boy. She didn't yet know Gienek's name.

She never heard another word about Jews.

Those Sunday afternoons, the men played cards: the boisterous, blond Jurek; the dapper, stylish Adam; the handsome, apple-cheeked Jozef, himself the owner of a large farm near Poznan; Staszek, with his marcelled hair; and Gienek, the carpenter from Lodz who had stood up for the Jews. Walenty didn't believe in card games.

There were only two girls: Magda, who worked at the Count's, and herself, Joanna. They talked. Every week Magda confided in her about her love for Jurek who had promised to divorce his wife after the war and marry her. "Can I believe him?" asked Magda. And every week Joanna tried to quiet Magda's doubts. At six o'clock, their Sundays ended: they had to get back for the evening milking.

She already milked quickly and skillfully. In the spring the cows were put to pasture. Every morning, noon, and evening, she would walk with Janek to a distant meadow. The hand cart full of milk cans clattered on the cobblestones, and the cans rattled. The same rattle and clatter could be heard all over town. The cows approached slowly across the fragrant meadow and waited patiently to be freed of the weight of their milk. She got to like their sad, sorrowful gazes. They had human names; one of them was called Hedwig.

She was in no hurry to get back. "Slowly," she would tell Janek. "The day is long, there's enough work ahead of us. Let the old lady wait." She would offer him one of the cigarettes Gienek brought her. Happy, Janek would lie down on the ground and puff away, and she too would smoke. Fragrant meadow, fragrant wind. She had come to love nature and to feel close to it, as she never had before. She felt a desire for colors, smells; suddenly her hunger for beauty stirred. She considered such feelings undignified, a betrayal of those she'd left behind in Poland.

With spring, the young men's gazes grew lingering, and expectant. Watching the cocks in the barnyard, the handsome, apple-cheeked Jozef would sigh and say, "Roosters are lucky. Jump on one, jump on the next," and he would laugh his good-natured, booming laugh. Now she often spoke about being faithful to her fiancé in Poland, and of their great love. She had a long conversation about this with Gienek. Magda whispered reproachfully in her ear, "Why are you such a saint? You're stupid. We should take what we can. Spring's the time for love."

One night Walenty surprised her with a visit. It was late, she was already in bed. A little pale, smelling of lily-of-the-valley soap, he appeared in her doorway. She asked, "What if someone acted like this with your wife, late at night? What would you say about that?" For a few days he walked around hurt.

In the evenings, on her way to her upstairs room, she would pause for a moment outside the door of the master's bedroom. She listened. The voice of a radio announcer was muffled and unclear. The clock ticked loudly. "Heavy fighting." Where was this heavy fighting taking place? Was it still near Stalingrad? She couldn't hear. She had no access to newspapers. She asked Walenty, but he didn't know much, and she didn't want to ask too many questions about matters that Joanna shouldn't be too interested in.

One night, listening through the door, she heard the second movement of Beethoven's Seventh. She hurried to her room. Because of the music she was choked up all evening. Her room was the only place she could lock the door and be alone, without Joanna.

She wrote at a little table near the window; outside was the barn gate, which, during the night was black and not blue (every morning she would look at the gate and think of the sea). She wrote letters to Jadwiga, sometimes to Anna. She wrote letters to Marian and to Father, and having written them, tore them to pieces. She kept a kind of diary, and hid her jottings under a loose floorboard; she put a chair on top of the board, and on top of the chair a washbasin and a pitcher. Later, she had to destroy these notes.

As soon as she'd arrived, she'd sent a letter to Halinka with her and Jadwiga's new addresses. Three months had passed since then, but there had been no word from Halinka. In the evenings, she would think about this silence.

She feared it more than she feared some of the images that floated through her mind and sometimes filtered into her dreams. She fell asleep quickly, exhausted, always with her arms hanging off the narrow mattress, stiff, dead as wood.

*

In the spring—probably it was April—Jadwiga received a letter from Father. The return address was that of the headmaster of the elementary school at Z.

After the war, we learned that it was the second letter Father wrote us. The first one, a farewell letter, was never sent. Father wrote it after leaving his hiding place in the family crypt of the Ukrainian beekeeper, where the beekeeper had moved him from the cellar in which his bees wintered over. He told Father he would come once a week with an adequate supply of food, and locked the cast-iron gate of the crypt. When he opened it—two weeks later— he found Father still alive, but completely emaciated. After that, Father slept in barns, one night here, one night there, trying in vain to find a permanent hiding place.

In one of these barns, he wrote us the farewell letter, and wrote another letter to his friend the schoolmaster, asking him to help him find a hiding place. "I won't blame you," he wrote, "if you can't do what I am asking. The risks are enormous. But you have to promise me that after the war you will give the enclosed letter to my daughters."

Having read the letter, which was delivered to him by a young shepherd boy, the director of the elementary school wrote back: "Give me five days." Together with his friend, a former senator from the Peasants' Party, he found Father a place in the countryside and ripped up the farewell letter.

"Dearest Jadwiga: I think of you day and night with love and longing, and like a wanderer in the desert thirsting for water, I yearn for the moment we will meet again. I am now living in the country, nourished by fresh milk and good rye bread," he wrote from his underground shelter.

When I opened Jadwiga's letter, this sheet, covered with the familiar, tall boxy handwriting, fell out of the envelope. (Margareta, the Schulzes' daughter, had brought me the letter. She threw it on the kitchen table, saying, "Do you think I'm your mailman, that I'll bring you your letters every day?") The ink was green, and those tall green letters kept jumping in front of my eyes like grasshoppers. I couldn't read a word. I ran out of the kitchen. For a long time I stayed in the stable, on the straw, reading Father's letter over and over.

Soon after, Jadwiga received a package from Z. We didn't know who sent it, but we immediately recognized what was inside: Aunt Stefania's slim navy dress. Nothing else. Aunt Stefania was sending us a signal: I am alive, I still exist.

What words could she have written? When she sent the dress—we never learned who helped her send it—she was still in the ghetto. But soon after, probably even before her signal reached us, she was gunned down in the field near the station, along with everyone else.

Halinka must have gotten our addresses to Z, probably through Agafia. Moved by Father's letter and by the sign from the ghetto, I didn't notice at first that Halinka hadn't written anything herself. And she was the only one who could have told me what was happening with Marian. Why did she choose to keep silent?

It wasn't until later that night that I suddenly understood why.

*

I went to visit Jadwiga. I was surprised that Schulz allowed me to make the trip, when he had always refused before, using every imaginable excuse; without the farmer's authorization, the police wouldn't issue a pass. Hearing that I was planning to visit a friend, Walenty announced he would go with me, unless, he added with a sneer, his company displeased me. I realized that his presence would ruin the meeting we had looked forward to for so long. It would make it impossible for us to talk freely, but I knew how sensitive and how easily hurt Walenty was. I didn't want—or was I afraid?—to offend him.

But it wasn't his presence, at least not *just* his presence, that ruined our meeting. We would surely have had a happy reunion anyway—Father's message was such good news— had not another letter arrived just before I went to see Jadwiga.

Actually the problem wasn't the letter, which was from Anna, but the blue envelope she had enclosed, addressed to Paulina, and bearing a handwritten notation. This envelope contained a letter Anna had sent to her cousin in the Sudeten mountains, and it had been returned. The notation, in small Gothic script (written by the farmer she worked for? by the local postman?) said, "*Paulina Kostecka zur Zeit Gestapo.*"

It took me a while to decipher the cramped little letters, but that one word—Gestapo—jumped right out at me. Before I even read the other words, I guessed their meaning. "Paulina Kostecka is now at the Gestapo." Anna had written that she couldn't read the notation on the envelope; she couldn't understand why the letter was returned.

My hand shook. My knees buckled and I sat down, and that moment has stayed just so in my memory: I see myself sitting at Klothilde Schulz's kitchen table with a blue envelope in my hand, bent over it, focused and attentive. Margareta is beside me, because it was she who, as usual, brought it to me and threw it on the table. On the floor is a bucket with potatoes I had just been peeling.

Gestapo! Immediately, instinctively, I thought, "Escape, escape," and this word stayed with me, nagging at me, as I traveled to see Jadwiga, with Walenty, all dressed up, riding beside me. It was the first time in two years that he had undertaken such a long trip: a whole hour by train.

So it was not just his presence that ruined our meeting, which should have been happy because of the news from Father—and which actually was so, in one sense, because Jadwiga had been *so* happy ever since she'd got Father's letter that nothing could dampen her exuberance. Not even the notation "*Paulina Kostecka zur Zeit Gestapo,*" not even the word "escape," which I flung at her immediately.

We were alone in her room, for a short time, just a few moments, because her mistress didn't allow guests in the rooms. "I don't think this has anything to do with us," she said.

"How could it not?" I asked. "Just think. Paulina was

supposed to send a package to the camp for Anna through a German acquaintance. Now if this German woman showed up there after our escape, it means . . ."

"It's been five months! Paulina could have been caught for a different reason. Most likely that's what happened. I don't think her arrest has anything to do with us. The Sudeten mountains are so far away."

Again she returned to the subject of Father's letter. She said it gave her strength. "You don't realize how much it helped me. You don't know how unhappy I've been here."

I knew how unhappy she'd been; she'd written about how her German mistress tormented her. But every letter ended, "Apart from that, I'm fine." And this statement had outweighed everything else. The important thing was: no one suspected her, neither the abominable German woman, nor Stefan the Pole, nor Branko the Serbian, nor Victor the Russian.

There were four slaves on the huge estate; the German woman's husband was in the army. Stefan managed the farm, and this saved Jadwiga, because he helped her and shielded her from the harassment. He was tall, strong, energetic; the German woman respected him and was afraid to lose him. His kind, friendly smile was like Gienek's.

Later, we all walked slowly, like peasants on a Sunday stroll, and had a desultory conversation about matters relating to the farm and the farmers. Jadwiga and I exchanged furtive glances that had to take the place of words. She looked haggard and very skinny in Aunt Stefania's slim, navy-blue dress. Her hands were the hands of an old, hard-working woman. Walenty and I walked back to the station alone. Jadwiga and Branko went to take care of the cows, Stefan and Victor to the horses. From a second-floor window the German woman watched us with hostility.

Walenty sat on the train, sulking. He didn't like Stefan. "And that friend of yours," he said, "she looks a little Jewish."

"I'll have to tell her that. She'll laugh," I replied.

*

I wrote to Anna, asking her to come. I wanted to talk to her. She arrived the next Sunday, looking a little unwell, but still beautiful. To my amazement, she shared Jadwiga's opinion; and she spoke practically the same words:

"Poor Paulina! But this has nothing to do with us. Besides, the Sudeten mountains, they're so far away." No, she didn't think we should run away. She thought I was overreacting.

I was relieved to hear her say this. The word "escape" began to fade from my thoughts, and one day I realized: it was gone.

That was the Sunday when, as Anna and I parted at the train station, Walenty said the words I never forgot: "Why is she hugging and kissing you as if you two were never going to see each other again?"

*

So Anna and Jadwiga were right. Three weeks had passed since the letter to Paulina was returned. I no longer thought about it. Only once I dreamed that I was sitting under a weeping willow on the bank of our little river, and Anna appeared with the blue envelope in her hand. "*Zur Zeit Gestapo*," she said loudly in German and kept walking in her elegant blue coat. The river reflected the blue sky, and took on its color, and suddenly I noticed that it was not the river but the barn door outside the window of my room.

I sensed a note of alarm in Klothilde's morning bell. She stood in the doorway, near the stairs, her lips pursed in a thin line. Klothilde rarely showed anger, and if she did, it was quiet and ironic. Our relationship was cool but correct. I never tried to charm her, and she never raised her voice. She was cold but just. But now she was shouting, "What do you think you're doing? Don't you know you're not allowed to have any visits at night? Especially from men!"

I had no idea what was she talking about.

"Nobody visits me at night. Nobody, ever."

"Don't lie!"

"I'm not lying," I cried indignantly.

"And who was it last night under your window? Who was calling? Who whistled? Who were you waiting for?"

I looked at her, genuinely amazed. Was she out of her mind? Was she dreaming?

"Maybe you dreamt it. No one was calling me; no one was whistling. I was asleep all night."

"Dreamt it? Herr Schulz ran out to the yard, but your visitor ran away. We both heard him run off toward the street."

*

It was a stuffy, hot day. Yellow-gray clouds filled the sky. Humidity rose from the earth.

We went out to the fields right after lunch.

"No doubt there will be a storm," predicted Walenty, pointing to a swarm of tiny flies spinning in the air. "We'll get good and wet, thanks to this shitty work."

The Schulzes and Margareta were far ahead of us on the road. They were walking briskly, energetically, with hoes over their shoulders. We dragged ourselves sleepily behind them, deaf to their calls.

"Let them yell." Janek mocked them. "We'll go slowly. We're no fools."

"You sound so brave when you're with us, but when push comes to shove, you shit in your pants." Walenty laughed.

Janek didn't answer. It was an accepted fact; Walenty was always right, and arguing with him was pointless, because things always went his way. I often felt sorry for the half-witted, good-hearted Janek who understood nothing but his need for sleep and the hunger in his belly. He and Walenty had lived in the same room for three years and were still as foreign to each other as on the first day. Walenty was not particularly pleased by the half-witted company; it was beneath his dignity to be friends with a "draught horse"—Janek used to drive a coach in a resort town, and he often boasted about it.

"He's always like this," Walenty said. "He complains, he bitches, but they scare the hell out of him! It's easy to be tough in Polish, when they can't understand you."

Janek said, "I can't talk German like you can."

"So why don't you learn? Look at Joanna. She's only been here five months, and she's already starting to speak

German. And you? You only know enough to ask the old man for tobacco, or to call '*Scheisse!*' when you're in the fields and have to take a shit."

The road led around the side of a hill. Further down, a factory and its smoke could be seen, and further still, among the meadows, flowed the Ruhr. The fields and forest took on ripe, moist colors. You could feel the spring turning into summer.

"When I get angry enough, I'm going to the factory. They quit at six. You can get enough sleep, not like here —cleaning under cows' tails and eating this shitty food."

"I don't go looking under cows' tails," Walenty answered proudly. He disdained our work in the cowshed.

"Cows or horses, what's the difference?" I said.

"What's the difference? My dear, have you . . . ?"

I preferred not to continue this discussion about the relative hierarchy of cowshed versus stable. (Besides, I thought I had already penetrated to the heart of such mysteries.) I was in a calm, good mood. Three weeks had passed since the arrival of the blue envelope with the Gothic writing. Anna and Jadwiga were right: Paulina's arrest had nothing to do with us.

There were yellow flowers beside the road. I would pick some and put them in my room. We could already see the field. It was very large, lined with rows of young beet greens, and reached all the way to the forest. Klothilde and Margareta were on their knees, thinning the plants. Schulz stood waiting, with sacks tied around his knees. He was furious, cursing under his breath.

We were always late getting to the fields. At first they

threw fits and yelled, but when they saw that it did no good, they contented themselves with low, angry mumbling.

I tied the old sacks around my knees with a string. A few large drops of rain fell—harbingers of a storm.

"*Herrgott*, move faster, damn it! Walenty and Janek, you go with the mistress! Joanna, you follow me!"

This was something new—all three of us were surprised.

"Be careful the old lady doesn't beat you up," laughed Walenty.

"You're a fool," I answered mechanically.

Until now, the three of us had always worked together: Walenty, Janek, and I. What did this new variation mean? I had a little lump of anxiety in my throat. I knelt obediently next to Schulz. The men and the two women were about fifteen yards away.

I carefully pulled out the clumps of young beets, leaving two or three of the healthiest-looking seedlings. They needed room—*Lebensraum!*—to grow into large, fat beets which would be taken to the cellar in the fall. In the fall! What would happen in the fall? Who knew? The rain was still sparse and fine; the dirt was soft. I was creeping on all fours, and my hands and knees left deep imprints. Schulz had stopped working and was watching me.

"Tell me, Joanna, this friend of yours, the one who came for a visit recently—what's her name? Anna? She's Jewish, isn't she?"

I looked him straight in the eye, amused by the question. Each time this scenario repeated itself, my first response was always the same: amusement.

"What?" I planted my hands firmly on the ground to hide their trembling.

"This Anna, she's a Jew, *eine Jüdin*. You understand what I'm saying, don't you?"

"What are you saying?" I answered, in a hurt voice. "Anna *nix Jude*."

"And the other one—she's also Jewish. You escaped together, right?"

"Yes, I already explained. We fled from a transport."

"Maybe it wasn't a transport—maybe it was a camp attached to a factory?"

"Not a camp. We fled from a transport."

"Well . . . you're a light blonde, Joanna, but . . ."

I stared back at him. "But what?" I looked, as always, bemused, and a little surprised. Schulz went back to his work. The conversation was over.

I pulled out the little beets and started singing at the top of my lungs. "Why so loud?" called Walenty. I was loud because I wanted to scream. Like in the camp, like in the camp. And through the pounding of my heart, through the throbbing in my ears, I felt a simple, child-like sorrow, and I wanted to cry. They had found out. It hadn't worked. It was all for nothing. Everything was ruined.

And then a sudden revelation: last night under my window, it had been Anna. It was she who whistled. She wanted to warn me, to let me know. *Paulina Kostecka zur Zeit Gestapo*, Anna's address in the Gestapo's hands. The Gestapo's mills grind slowly, but surely. My first impulse —to run away—had been the right one. I shouldn't have given in to the argument that the Sudeten mountains were far away and that Paulina had nothing to do with us.

Klothilde had said they were heavy male steps. Perhaps it was a messenger from Anna? It didn't matter. Someone wanted to warn me, to tell me.

I was already calm. I sang "Otchitchorniya" and I could hear Walenty say to Klothilde: "Joanna is happy, Joanna's in love," and for the first time I was grateful to him.

*

The rain chased us out of the field. It came violently, smelling of spring. The smell was suffocating. We were running, soaked, dripping with water.

"What did the old man want from you?"

"He said he had to watch me because I was lazy."

"And that was why you were laughing so much?"

"Sure, let him watch me."

As I ran, I put together a plan. We would escape the next day. Luckily, the next day was Sunday. In the afternoon I'd go to Jadwiga's and leave with her from there. Today I had to find some shoes for Jadwiga. I had a coupon for one pair of wooden shoes, but she couldn't travel in wooden shoes. I had to convince the shoemaker to sell me leather shoes. I'd managed to convince him once before; my dark red pumps proved it. So maybe I could do it again. Maybe I could do it again? I *had* to do it. Jadwiga had to have leather shoes for the journey, and she would have them— shoes for the long journey to who knows where. I didn't know how to find out whether Anna really had escaped.

We couldn't leave her to fend for herself. But what if I was wrong? What if it wasn't Anna—or someone sent by her —whistling under my window? There was no way I could find out.

Running through the rain, I thought: Stop lying to yourself, you know there's a way to find out, you've known it for some time: Gienek. You can't do it alone, but you can ask Gienek, he's the only one you can ask, the only one who stood up for the Jews during that first visit to Magda and Jurek. Even then you told yourself: Remember that boy. Despite everything he has remained your friend, despite that long conversation about love, despite your refusal . . . Stop lying to yourself.

So I started thinking: Gienek will help me. I would tell him the truth, I didn't want to lie to him. For the first time, I decided to break our most sacred rules, to let someone in on our secret. Perhaps I was too weak to bear one more blow alone.

On Saturdays we could quit work earlier. We had already finished dinner. I had already done the dishes. The sun was shining after the rain.

I heard music and Klothilde's *Plattdeutsch* from the farmers' room. Margareta was curling her hair for Sunday. There was a fire in the bathroom stove to heat water for the family bath, which they would take, one by one, in the same water.

I'd always liked those Saturday evenings, with their promise of Sunday's leisure; but now, all at once, they seemed hateful, the coziness and calm suddenly repulsive.

I sat in my room without moving, without thinking. The slamming of a door roused me from my stupor. Schulz was going out. Where was he headed? And for what reason? He never used to leave the house on Saturday evening. I took Jadwiga's letters out of my drawer and got my notes and a notebook from under the loose floorboard. I tore them into little pieces and threw them into the latrine in the cowshed.

Later I informed Klothilde that I was going to the shoemaker's to pick up some shoes.

The wizened old shoemaker had a good reputation among the Poles; they said you could always come to some kind of understanding with him. That day, however, he told me it was impossible. But traveling in wooden clogs was definitely a bad idea. "Oh, Herr Joseph!" I cried. "Have you forgotten how high the heels are on those beautiful, dark red pumps? Have *you* ever tried to wear high heels after a day of hard work?"

Old Joseph laughed at my joke. Hah, hah, are all Poles so witty? He resisted a little longer, but finally he reached under the counter. "But this is the last time!"

Back in the street, I took a few steps toward the farm where Gienek worked—and turned back. No, I wouldn't drag him into our affairs. It must have been Anna. Who else could it have been? Suddenly I imagined a policeman waiting for me in Klothilde's kitchen, and it made the shoebox seem ludicrous.

From an alley came the sound of Gienek's voice. "Where are you going? Wait!" He was on his way back from the fields. He walked with a springy gait: tall, strong, relaxed. I showed him the shoes; he whistled appreciatively.

"Great. You can wear them tomorrow. We'll go for a walk."

I didn't answer, so he asked, "What's wrong?"

"Nothing."

"You can't fool me. Did you have a fight with the old lady? Don't pay it any mind."

"I didn't have a fight with anybody."

"But something is bothering you, I can see it. Tell me, maybe I can help you, you know that I . . ."

"Come tonight to the ravine behind the gardens, and I'll tell you."

"Something serious?"

There was concern in his voice.

*

I opened the window in my room. The perfume of the night-blooming stock in the gardens blew in on the breeze.

I had another hour until my meeting with Gienek. I lay down on the bed and was overcome by the memory of our final days in the camp, the memory of waiting. We had lain helpless on our bunks, experienced our deaths in every moment of despair, and our resurrections with every new glimmer of hope. But then we were all together, and now I was alone. Jadwiga was alone, too, and this loneliness was hard to bear.

I jumped up. Schulz had returned. He had come back alone. I heard his loud voice from downstairs. He was describing something to Klothilde. Margareta laughed loudly. The radio stopped playing. The footsteps stopped. They went to sleep.

I tiptoed down the stairs. The door that led through the stable to the barn was locked. I ran my hand along the beam against the wall. I was right: the key was in the corner furthest from the door. I turned back and went to the room where the men slept. Janek lay on his bed, staring at the ceiling, smoking a pipe. I envied him this relaxed idleness. Walenty was writing a letter. He put down his pencil when he saw me.

"Have a seat. Why didn't you come earlier? Everyone was here, but they've already gone home."

"I'm going out for an hour. I wanted to ask you—"

"You're going out? That's something new. What about your fiancé?" he sneered. I pretended not to hear him.

"You know, the old man locked the door to the yard, but I found the key. Please lock it after I leave. I'll call out when I come back."

"You say he locked the door? What a bastard! That's something else new."

In the ravine, I sat down on an uprooted tree and waited.

The sky was clear, sprinkled with stars; the smell of rain still hung in the air. What would I say to Gienek? How was I going to tell him? Suddenly I regretted what I had done. I didn't feel up to this confession. I feared the words I would have to say.

He hurried over, sat down, put his arm around me.

Before he could ask anything, I said, "You know, I'm Jewish."

"So?"

I had been prepared for shock, for embarrassment, for an uncomfortable silence, for everything except these ordinary, normal words. The tension of the last few hours suddenly broke. I bit my lips—more than anything, I didn't want to cry.

"So what if you're Jewish?"

I told him everything. He listened carefully, without interrupting, and with mounting astonishment. The smile faded from his face—at last he understood. He bridled when I told him that all I was asking him was to find out if Anna had escaped.

"Don't talk nonsense, and don't be childish," he cried. "I'll go to Anna's. I'll also go to Jadwiga's. I will go, not you. You can't. For me it's nothing."

In the morning he would go to Anna's, and in the afternoon to Jadwiga's, and he would tell her to be at the train station in the evening, ready for the trip. He was in no danger at all, he said, and he even enjoyed the adventure.

And then he asked if this fiancé of mine really existed, or if I had made him up just as I had Katarzyna and Joanna.

I walked back along the gardens. The scent of night-blooming stock and reseda perfumed the air. I opened the gate very carefully and walked silently across the yard. From underneath the men's window—their room was in the farm part of the property, far away from the Schulzes' apartment—I called Walenty. He came down at once.

He was angry. "Where have you been, girl, in the middle of the night? Be careful, I warn you, you'll end up in trouble."

Without taking off my clothes, I threw myself onto the bed. There was only one more day. I must get my dress ready and remove the stains from my coat, which still bore the traces of our nights in the woods. We would go south, as far as we could, to the lake near the Swiss border.

If the police didn't show up before then. Always that little word: if.

*

At noon, on my way to the meadow with Janek, I noticed Gienek. He was walking along, whistling, with his hands in his pockets. I thought that he must have changed his mind, that he couldn't—or didn't want to—go. And I felt a pang in my stomach.

"Joanna, look who's coming," Janek said happily. "That means cigarettes!"

Gienek announced that he was on his way to the pasture to see whether the grass was ready to be scythed. Since he'd run into us, though, he'd sit with us a moment. He was in no hurry.

I sat down beside a cow, a bucket between my legs. Gienek reclined nearby on the grass. We waited a while, until Janek, happy with his Sulima cigarette, wandered off.

I said, "You couldn't go, right?"

"Anna's escaped. She isn't there."

The cow kicked and switched her tail angrily: a quick, nervous spasm of my fingers had hurt her.

"Were you there?"

"No, I wasn't. At the station I met someone I know. He volunteered the information. I didn't even have to ask. After all, it's news."

"What did he say?"

"He said that there was a girl in their village who was working for the wealthiest farmer, but she had packed up and run away. Apparently she was Jewish. The police were looking for her. She was really pretty, he said, didn't look Jewish at all."

First, there had been six of us, then four, then three, then . . . I told myself to stop. "What is this stupid counting for? You know she's run away. You just wanted to check, to have a clear conscience."

Anna was not given to shows of tenderness; on the contrary, she was rather cool. But that afternoon, at the train station, at the last moment, when the train was already pulling into the platform . . . The reddish sparks in her hair, and Walenty's words, prophetic and ominous, that we were saying goodbye as if we'd never see each other again. Why never? I knew: never.

"You expected as much. So what's the problem?" said Gienek.

I really didn't know what the problem was. Maybe it was that I hadn't tried hard enough to convince Anna and Jadwiga, but instead had let them convince me. It had been easier, more convenient. And now it was late—maybe too late.

The cow kicked the bucket over, and milk spilled out and quickly soaked into the ground.

"I'll be waiting in the ravine tonight at eight. Don't worry. Everything will work out."

Janek returned. Each of us smoked one more cigarette.

"Gienek's a devil of a guy," mused Janek on the way back. "He doesn't work too hard. He smokes good cigarettes. All the girls like him."

Klothilde questioned me in detail: Was I planning to go out in the afternoon? It was Sunday, after all. Where was I going? To Niederwiesen. With Walenty? With Walenty. She said: "You are to be back exactly at six." As if I couldn't escape before six . . .

On the grounds of the Count's estate, the rhododendrons were in bloom. The lawns were soft as carpets. Jurek set up a table in front of his little cottage. The sun was warm. The men were playing cards, warming themselves in the sun. Everything seemed the same as it did every Sunday, and yet it was different. It was not Joanna's eyes that were watching, not Joanna's ears that were listening. The jovial laughter, the crude jokes, the same old conversations, the simple Sunday leisure of farmhands and slaves. The lucky ones!

Magda said, "Did Adam write to you?"

I said, "He did."

"He likes you. Do you like him?"

How would Adam react if I told him? But I could never tell him. "There's something strange about you," he had said. "I don't know how to describe it. You're odd . . ." No, I didn't want to know how he would react.

"I can't understand why you're so untouchable. It just

isn't normal. Has he already written that he loves you?"

"No."

"Will you tell me when he does?"

"I will. If I tell anyone, it'll be you."

I thought: I could tell you the truth. You're a good, decent girl to whom nothing matters but love. Joanna likes you a lot. But you have a big mouth, and that Jurek of yours believes that the only good thing about Hitler is, well, you know . . .

"You're lucky. Gienek has a crush on you, too. But, between you and me, Adam is better looking. I guess I like mustaches . . ."

Magda squinted in the mild sun. The wind blowing in from the Ruhr lifted her fine hair. Her full, pink face with its tiny eyes resembled a sweet little marzipan pig. I was sorry I had to ask her to pay me back the money I had lent her. All I had was thirty marks, and who knew how much Jadwiga had.

"Joanna, dear, I can pay you after the first. I've bought two plaid shirts for Jurek. You know how angry he was, he even raised his hand to me . . . because Jurek . . ."

I walked back with Staszek, who was proud of how he'd marcelled his hair for the summer. Fortunately, he was not a talkative sort, and the only sentence he uttered concerned the war: "They say the Krauts are getting their asses kicked."

*

Work was over. The kitchen had been scrubbed. Near the door stood a row of freshly scoured milk cans I would no longer have to carry. Now for a brief farewell visit to the men. They would find out tomorrow.

I was too nervous to sit down, I just stood there, smoking a cigarette. Gienek must have come back already. In two hours I would meet Jadwiga, we would board the train . . .

"Tomorrow the old man's going to Iserlohn," said Walenty. "We'll be able to take it easy."

Schulz was going to the *Arbeitsamt* to bring home a new worker.

"Well, I'll see you tomorrow," I said and left quickly. They would find out tomorrow.

I put on a new dress, braided my hair, and pinned the braids up on my head. I took Jadwiga's shoes, my coat, and my handbag with the half-horseshoe and the thirty marks. In the loft, I moved the ladder over to the opening where we threw the hay down, and I went straight to the stable, avoiding the kitchen and the farmer's living quarters which adjoined it. I went up the steps from the yard to the path alongside the gardens. From there I could see the Schulzes' entire place, as if it were a scene painted on china. The evening was bright and clear, and in the lighted window, I caught a glimpse of Janek in his white shirt.

Gienek was already waiting. He sat on a tree trunk, in the same spot where he had listened to my confession yesterday. He had not heard my footsteps. When I touched his shoulder, he jerked away, as if he had been burned. I knew right away that something had happened. I thought despairingly that they had taken Jadwiga away, that he had arrived too late.

"She's very sick. She can't travel in this condition. The police were by to see her." He spoke softly, as if it were I and not Jadwiga who was ill; his tone of voice annoyed me.

"Tell it to me from the very beginning," I said drily. He stared at me in surprise, and, when he continued to sit there in silence, I added angrily, "Go on. I'm listening."

Gienek hadn't seen Jadwiga. But he had talked to Stefan, who knew everything. She was sick and had a high fever; she couldn't eat, couldn't drink. She had collapsed. Stefan was helping her with the harder chores. She had to hide how sick she was. She had to keep working.

Soon after she fell ill, the police arrived. The German woman called her, "Come here, you damned Jew." Two men from the Gestapo were waiting in the yard. Stefan overheard the German woman's conversation with the police. Only because of her pleas did they agree to leave Jadwiga until the *Arbeitsamt* sent another girl. "*Einige Tage*—a few days," she'd begged.

They left, taking with them Jadwiga's identification card. As soon as they were gone, the German woman notified the *Arbeitsamt*. "You damned Jew," she said to Jadwiga.

I was silent, petrified. We would never get out of this.

"Stefan said that he'd come on Wednesday night and tell us when Jadwiga would be able to run away."

Three days. We'd never get out.

"She has to force herself," I said.

"She's very sick, believe me . . ."

"She has to find the strength, she *has* to."

"Calm down."

The Journey

I wanted to explain to Gienek that I wasn't angry with him, nor with Jadwiga. Only when we were almost at the garden gate did I apologize to him. "What would I have done without you?" I said, more to myself than to him. The smell of reseda and night-blooming stock was just like at our house on the riverbank. Only the frogs weren't croaking. The light was still on in the room where the men slept.

Just one hour of sleep, I thought. Then I'll calmly think everything through. I still believed in the miraculous power of sleep.

From the yard, I could hear someone laughing—it was Walenty, teasing me, asking why I needed my coat when I went out on dates. Couldn't my boyfriend keep me warm?

*

The days were filled with a kind of double waiting: waiting for news of Jadwiga and waiting for the police. I made myself get through the time, as if I were trudging through a snow drift: step by step, hour by hour, not a moment of rest from the hard labor of waiting, except perhaps at night. It felt safer at night, because why would they go to the trouble when they could be sleeping? At night I reasoned: Perhaps they were also letting Schulz keep me until he got a new worker. But by dawn I was telling myself that, one way or the other, they would come, if for no other reason than to ask me the same questions they'd asked Jadwiga. And I would resume my waiting. Still, I would run downstairs cheerfully, eagerly load the cans onto the cart, milk the cows, feed the pigs, and crawl among the rows of beets, not even feeling the pain in my back that Janek and Walenty complained about after a few hours of work—it was still the season for thinning. The hard physical work was a relief; it distracted me from my worries.

I recall one image from those days of difficult waiting: the train in the meadow. It was on a day when a thunderstorm was brewing. Under the black, rain-swollen clouds we were raking hay in the fields. A long, serpentine train slithered through the meadow. Watching it disappear from sight, I felt—very clearly, very palpably—the proximity of danger and the futility of my desperate scrambling, my frantic efforts to break out of this closed circle. It was as if a metal band was suddenly squeezing my ribs. The world went quiet and dark. A thick, heavy silence fell. I dropped my rake on the ground, loosened my blouse. I was gasping for breath.

*

Unexpectedly, Magda returned my money. I asked Gienek to go to "his" German and buy two hats and two pairs of gloves. This German was accustomed to selling Gienek various items for his sister, who worked in a factory near Berlin, so there was no danger that these new purchases would arouse suspicion. The thin leather gloves he brought were the same beige color as the informer's, and, like the beret, very elegant. Gienek promised to deliver a large straw hat in a few days. He was smiling. The hats amused him. The pity had disappeared from his voice.

*

On Wednesday night I sneaked out of the house through the stable window. I didn't want to ask the men to close and open the door. I knew I would come back late.

I struggled with the window for a long time. Then I used some grass to scrub the manure from my shoes. Gienek and I walked down the footpath that led along the train track. Stefan was supposed to come that way and then return, as quickly as possible, to the train station, in time to catch the last train. It was dark. The path was overgrown; obviously it was seldom used. We walked rapidly, so that Stefan wouldn't have so far to go. A cigarette flashed in the darkness, like a firefly, and then we heard him, hurrying, panting.

He grabbed my arm and said, "She's still too weak. She can barely stand. She wrote you a letter."

From his pocket he took a sheet of paper folded in quarters. It was too dark for me to read. "It's not going to work out," I thought. I was cold.

"She's asking you not to wait for her."

In the flare of a match I caught his anxious, questioning gaze.

"Tell her that the day after tomorrow I'll be waiting for her at 10:00 P.M. at the train station, and that she has to come. She must."

I was dizzy from the cigarette and the darkness. He shook his head no. "It's out of the question. You have no idea how . . ."

"So then, when?"

"On Sunday. On Sunday it will also be easier to sneak out of the house. Will you wait?"

"On Sunday . . . 4:00 P.M. . . . at the station. Do you promise?"

"I promise."

I held both his hands tightly. I kept repeating, "Stefan, Stefan, thank you, thank you . . ."

We were on our way back. I was still cold.

"Can you hear the crickets chirping?" I asked Gienek, but he didn't answer. Nor did he say, as he usually did, "Don't worry." Instead, he left rapidly, without a word.

Back in my room, I didn't turn on the light, but lit a match to read Jadwiga's letter. "Dear Joanna: Go without me. You can't wait any longer. Escape! You'll be with Father, I'll be with Mother. Good luck. Thank you for everything."

I covered my face with a pillow and wept.

*

Walenty immediately brought us the news he had overheard: they had been allotted an additional worker, a Russian woman. She was supposed to arrive next week.

*

On Sunday, I woke up long before dawn. The sea-blue barn gate was still black. I had only slept for an hour. I dreamed that Jadwiga was sitting on the narrow bench at Halinka's and saying, "Go without me. She doesn't want me."

Soon, at four in the afternoon, we would meet at the train station. Stefan had promised. I counted the days and couldn't get over my surprise: it had only been a week. I looked in the mirror, amazed not to find any trace of the week's anxiety. I had lost weight, but that was all.

On my way to the pasture I warned Janek that I would be late for the evening milking. I would come straight to the meadow. He gave me a conspiratorial wink and laughed.

"I want you to know, Joanna, that I'm not like Walenty. It's none of my business. But people shouldn't use the kind of words he uses."

"What words?"

"He never said anything bad about you before. But now . . . 'Goddamnit,' he says, 'every night she's screwing someone and then she yells for us to open the door.' He's probably angry it isn't him."

Lunch consisted of sweet beer soup. After a few spoonfuls I ran to the cowshed and threw up.

I sang loudly, perhaps too loudly, as I washed the dishes. I scrubbed the kitchen counter until it shone like a mirror and swept the kitchen floor. It was one-thirty in the afternoon.

In the drawer of my table I left an unfinished letter without an address. "My dear friend, I'm telling you, when I finally get angry enough, I'm just going to run away. I slave here from dawn till dusk. I'm fed up with the beets and the cows. I have a friend in Leipzig, she promised to get me a job in a restaurant. I'm not sure yet . . ."

I wrote another letter, to Gienek, and took that one with me.

I walked carefully down the stairs. Eighteen steps—I had counted them when I scrubbed them that first day. I paused outside the Schulzes' bedroom. Everything was quiet. The clock was ticking. They were resting after their Sunday lunch.

As usual, I went out into the yard through the stable window, and then down the same road I had been taking at night, along the gardens. The gardens were magnificent; they were in full bloom.

Gienek wasn't there yet. I stretched out on the grass and shaded my eyes from the sun.

The first step is always the hardest . . . Later, everything has a certain momentum. You only have to cross the line beyond which there is no return. That's how it was in the ghetto, that's how it was in the camp, that's how it will be in an hour, at the train station. I was thinking this quite calmly, as if none of it concerned me, as if I weren't the one who would soon have to cross that line for the third time—I could have fallen asleep, I felt so nice and cozy lying on the grass.

A shadow blocked out the sun: Gienek stood above me. His voice shook, and his hand felt clammy when he touched me.

From his pocket he took a bottle of fruit wine. "You should have a drink for good luck."

"I can't. I'm sorry, I can't."

With Gienek's arrival, my nervousness returned. Again I had a lump in my throat.

"You have to. I stole this wine from the cellar especially to drink with you."

I took a swallow. It was sour and bitter.

"To your success!"

He tipped back his head. The wine gurgled in the bottle, and then, comically, in his throat.

"What about the hat?" I asked. The hat was very important, just as the kerchief had once been important, the kerchief with its bunches of red roses blooming among green leaves.

"I have it. I hid it in the bushes."

The hat was beautiful, made of fine brown straw; its wide brim was decorated with a nosegay of wildflowers.

I put it on, and Gienek laughed. He said, "You look like a real German." And I said, "*Zweimal Bonn bitte, dritte Klasse.*"

The train to Bonn via Cologne was leaving at 4:20 P.M.

The early afternoon was blazing hot. The sun burned our backs.

In a long-forgotten gesture, I held the brim of my hat to keep it from blowing away in the wind, which wasn't even blowing. I couldn't help noticing how the beige color of my gloves stood out against my tanned arms. I remembered my first hat—a present for my high school graduation—and how, looking at myself in the mirror, I'd lifted my hand to its white brim. Then, too, my arms were brown from the sun; sunlight filled the room and flooded the garden beyond the open door; from the garden, someone was calling, "Come to the river." It was a scorching day, just like this one . . .

We sat down, not far from the train station, under the

trestle. I took out my identification card and asked Gienek to destroy it after I left. Then I gave him my letter.

"You can protect yourself with this letter. It proves that you didn't know anything."

He laughed, and said, "Don't worry. I can take care of myself."

In the letter, I apologized to Gienek for having shamelessly deceived him and for leaving without saying goodbye. "The love I showed you was only a trick to get money for the journey. At the last moment, though, my conscience wouldn't let me do it. I must tell the truth: I don't love you, and I'm leaving you. I'm going to Leipzig, to a friend, but please don't tell anyone."

It was almost four. We had to go.

The square in front of the station was swarming with people. The townspeople were coming to spend Sunday in the country. Yellow umbrellas shaded the tables of the outdoor café. People were eating ice cream.

Stefan came out of the station with the first wave of travelers. He was alone. Tense and serious, he walked toward us. He had promised to bring Jadwiga, and yet he was alone.

The sun went out. I grabbed Gienek's arm. "It can't be," he muttered. Just then I noticed her. They were approaching separately. I was frightened by how much she had changed: the pained face, the ashen complexion, her stockings hanging in twisted rolls around her skinny legs. I wanted to weep, but there was no time; there was no time for anything. We kissed each other decorously, coolly.

"Why did you bring all these things?" I hissed angrily, pointing to a small bundle in her hand. I was afraid to look at her. One tender word, one careless gesture, and we would both fall apart. Her lips were chapped, her eyes glazed. She was running a fever.

Stefan had managed to sneak her into the woods, where she had changed clothes. They were afraid to board the train in their village. Instead they walked through the forest to the next station. She barely made it.

"He saved my life," said Jadwiga, and repeated it again, this time to Stefan. "You saved my life."

But there was no time for any of that, neither for thanks nor for emotion. We said goodbye quickly, in frantic, anxious haste, exchanging pitiful incomplete phrases: "For everything . . . for everything . . . if it weren't for you . . ."

They walked away. "*Zweimal Bonn bitte, dritte Klasse.*" With my gloved hand—the glove that was the same beige color as the informer's—I took the tickets from the revolving plate and whispered to Jadwiga, "Let's go."

We stepped onto the waiting train. From then on, Jadwiga would be Barbara Falenska, and I would become Maria Walkowska. We kept our real birthdays, and our real place of birth. There was no time to invent new biographies.

The train. Bright sunshine, a curtain of light dense as fog. My memory is blinded by all that brightness. Very little remains from the first leg of the trip: Jadwiga sitting beside the door in a crowded compartment, and me, by the window. I can see the hat I wore, probably because it was so important; I'm convinced that it was because of the hat and the gloves that the ticket clerk did not ask for identification. That's all, the rest has slipped away, my memory is blind and deaf until (after one hour? two hours?) a river appears—I seem to have a fondness for rivers. I recall the German words that went through my mind when I saw the river: *Das ist der Rhein*, that is the Rhine, an echo of the words that once described another river: *Das ist die Ruhr*. I can also see the two undercover agents near the stairs leading to the underpass at the train station in Cologne, where we changed trains for Bonn.

There's not a trace of the great cathedral, even though it must have appeared outside the train windows and then disappeared just as quickly. I know, because I checked it many years later.

But the two agents are very clear. They stand there, searching the faces of the passersby. I also see clearly a man with long sideburns, probably a Frenchman, whom they stopped. I can still hear my voice, at the moment we passed them, saying, "*Heute ist es aber schwül*," it's so humid today, because I was in a cold sweat.

I painstakingly pronounced the word *schwül*. "Not *schwil, schwü-ül*," my German teacher used to say. "You, of all people, should hear the difference, with your ear for music." She was a good but demanding teacher who three times failed Ivan on his finals; later, when Ivan joined the SS, she fled to a different city, fearing his revenge. *Heute ist es aber schwü-ül*. I lifted my hand to the brim of my hat, and, with that relaxed, slightly artificial gesture that called attention to the elegant detail of my wardrobe, walked past the secret policemen. Their jovial faces stayed in my memory.

That is the first complete scene from the trip south. I breathed a sigh of relief when we handed in our tickets at Bonn. From that moment on, no one could check where we'd come from. For a long time, and with some difficulty —I'd left my glasses on the train—I studied the timetable. In an hour, a train was leaving for Frankfurt; this destination suited our plan. I put on my gloves and went to the ticket office. I was able to sound natural, I'd had practice. And once again, the clerk did not ask for identification.

Then we left the station quickly, to get out of the

policemen's sight and to avoid unexpected conversations and questions.

There was a little park nearby. The sun was low. It was almost time for the evening milking. Janek would be waiting in the pasture, cursing. Klothilde would start to yell when she saw him dragging the milk cart home—alone, without me. Schulz would run to the police. And Stefan, amazed, would call out to the farmer's wife in the words we'd agreed on, "What do you mean, she isn't here? Where is she? She was lying in bed, too weak to get up." The German woman would make a telephone call: "The damned Jew has run away!"

Not a soul was in the park. Now we could tell each other everything, but the words came slowly, and soon stopped altogether. The silence deepened. Jadwiga's breath was heavy, hot; her stockings hung on her legs in twisted rolls. She said, "I thought I was going to die."

I sat motionless, averting my eyes from her skinny legs.

*

The train to Frankfurt was two hours late, so we left the station again. This time we went toward the center of the city. I said, "Perhaps we'll see the house where Beethoven was born. After all, this is Beethoven's birthplace." But when we found ourselves in the old narrow streets, I forgot all about Beethoven. I wanted to return to the station as soon as possible. I was afraid we might get lost, and that the train would leave without us.

It was getting dark. The platform was empty. The

train signals blinked on, then off. A cool evening breeze had begun to blow. Jadwiga rested her head on my shoulder, something she had never done before. You have to get well, I kept thinking. You have to.

A man and a woman sat down next to us and tried to strike up a conversation. It was clear that they were bored and were hoping that talking to us would make the waiting go faster. But we couldn't risk even the most innocent or casual conversation. Suddenly the woman seemed surprised. "Your accent is so unusual. You must not be from around here."

"I'm from Vienna."

"Oh, Viennese waltzes, they're so beautiful," said the man and, opening a black case I'd mistaken for a suitcase, took out an accordion. Standing in front of us, he played waltzes until the train arrived at the platform.

*

The train was empty, so it was easy to find an unoccupied compartment. Handing back our tickets, the female conductor said politely, "There's so much room, you ladies will be able to get some sleep." I pulled the curtains on the door. First, it was the river Ruhr, then the Rhine. Soon it would be the Main.

I laughed. Jadwiga was already asleep. Afraid that we might oversleep and be surprised by someone, I decided to stay awake. But sleep overcame me, too.

I had to struggle to rouse myself. Jadwiga was sitting up, extremely pale. Sleep seemed to have brought her fever down.

"Comb your hair," I said, "and clean your nails."
Looking into the black windowpane, we combed our tangled hair.

We arrived at four in the morning. The station was
dark, deserted, enormous. The emptiness and the dimmed
lights made it seem even larger. People rushed to the exit
and disappeared; the lobby was deserted. No one was arriving or leaving, nobody was waiting for a train except us.
We were as conspicuous as if we were on stage. We had to
get out of there as soon as possible, on the next train, but
the next train wasn't leaving until dawn.

I bought our tickets; they legitimized our presence in
the station at that hour. The sleepy clerk glared at us—no
one was buying tickets yet.

We walked down the stairs to the restroom. I thought
we would be safer there than in the empty lobby. For a
long time we sat on the dark-red plush sofa, among gleaming
mirrors that reflected our faces and figures. A thin trickle
of water murmured in the pipes. It was an inviting, elegant
place. The plush sofa was soft, but I couldn't stand the way
our images in the mirrors mocked our gestures, our expressions. It was unnerving. We went back to the huge lobby,
which was still deserted, and sat down on the least conspicuous bench, off in a corner.

I must have fallen asleep because suddenly I noticed
that we were not alone. Two young men were sitting beside
us. They sat with their chins resting on their chests, but
they were not asleep. I could guess that their thoughts were
the same as ours: Security police, identification papers,
train . . .

The Journey

The sound of a whistle pierced the silence. They stirred. One of them jumped up from the bench, as if his nerves had just snapped. His face told me everything, and his pale complexion was a sure sign of the rutabaga camp. The other one tugged at his sleeve. I distinctly heard him whisper, "It's not the right one." They were Russian. They looked at us: Had those girls heard? Their expressions mirrored ours—the same insecurity, fear, and hope.

But now we had to walk away.

A policeman suddenly confronted us as we crossed the empty lobby: "Papers, please." I heard his voice as if from a distance. My ears started buzzing, my knees went weak.

"Well, really." I heard my own voice, also as if from a distance. I sounded upset, and slightly ironic. What made me say that? Did I realize what I was saying? "Again? How many times an hour are we supposed to show our documents? Who do you think we are, sir? My husband is at the front! Perhaps you could direct us to the waiting room. We are traveling from Lübeck to Heidelberg, and we are extremely tired, completely exhausted . . . and this lady" —I pointed to Jadwiga—"is feeling absolutely wretched."

The words flowed out smoothly, fluently, as if I had spent my entire life speaking nothing but German. Where did I find that tone: offended, but calm, and convinced of being right? I don't know, I don't know.

"I thought you'd gone crazy." Jadwiga barely suppressed a nervous laugh. "My husband is at the front!" We sat hidden behind a huge crate in one of the side corridors off the large hall. Perhaps I really had gone crazy. I don't know.

The policeman had led us to the waiting room, as I'd requested. We waited there a while, but then fled the place; we were afraid he'd change his mind and come back. Hidden behind a crate, we covered our mouths with our hands to muffle the laughter that shook our bodies, the laughter we couldn't control.

We walked all over the beautiful city and along the river. We walked all day, from morning till evening, with a break for a nap. At night we returned to the castle hill to sleep. First we walked in the sunshine, then in the rain, and, at moments, especially when the sun was shining, it really felt as if we had come there only for sightseeing.

We liked Heidelberg immensely, from the moment we arrived. We liked it as we stood in the little square in front of the train station, even though we hadn't yet seen the town, only one street, shady, lined with trees still wet with early-morning dew. But even before we really saw the town, we sensed that it was different from the towns in the north. The air was different there, mild and very clean, but most importantly, the breeze was warm. I said to Jadwiga, who when we arrived was still Jadwiga but who was about to turn into Barbara: "See, I knew that it would be nice here, that's why I chose this town." She gave me a surprised look, much like the one she'd given me when I asked if she liked my hat. I went on talking, explaining that the town was famous for its old university and its wineries, as well as its river, which was the subject of quite a few folk songs.

"Come on," I said, "let's go see everything—the university, the river, the wineries, the castle hill."

"No doubt another Beethoven was born in this town, too?" said Jadwiga (still not Barbara), and I understood that she'd had enough of my enthusiasm. I remembered that she was ill. I fell silent but didn't stop smiling—because during our entire journey we were supposed to smile and look cheerful.

We walked straight down a wide, shady street, strolling like a couple of tourists. Jadwiga's pumps were too big for her, and her heels clacked against the pavement; the sound was getting on my nerves. I was also annoyed by the little bundle Jadwiga was clutching under her arm, her lace-up shoes—why in the world had she taken them along? I knew that she was wearing two dresses and three slips—she was so thin she could get away with it—and that irritated me as well. And even though I realized that neither the shoes nor the slips were the real reason for my anger, I couldn't stop being angry, and so we began our walk in an unfriendly silence.

Only when I looked at Jadwiga's face did my anger vanish. And that only made things worse, because anger gave way to tenderness, and now, more than ever, we could not afford to be tender or soft. I said, "We'll go up the hill, get some rest, and think about what to do next." She answered obediently, "All right." She agreed to everything. Her fever was up again, and she felt listless.

The Journey

We were walking along an empty street, under the damp green of the trees, in the morning sunshine, passing the façades of the sleeping houses. I felt my tiredness diminish with each step. I was enjoying the quiet morning, the safe emptiness of the streets. I even remembered another morning walk, very long ago, and the memory was so sudden and so distinct that this street seemed to be that other street, and this moment that other moment from the past.

I calmed down a little because we were now walking uphill which meant that at least we were heading in the right direction. Jadwiga was explaining to me in a whisper why she didn't want to part with her shoes, why she'd taken them with her. Her cheeks were on fire, her breath was hot.

Slowly, the empty street filled with people. They stepped solemnly from their houses, the men very stiff and formal in dark holiday suits; their wives matronly in proper hats and gloves; their children in knee socks, looking plump, well-fed. All were strolling in a dignified, ceremonious manner. Whitsuntide. The sonorous ringing of a bell dropped heavily into the morning silence, first one drop, then many more drops, and suddenly there was no more silence— only resonant, melodious bells.

The air smelled of acacias. A light breeze blew, most likely from the river, and the buildings along the street that climbed the hill gradually stopped looking like city buildings and nestled among the bushes and flowers of their manicured gardens. Higher up, there were no more houses, only greenery on both sides of the road. As we rounded a curve, the sky spread out before us, and then I saw the town. It was even more beautiful than I had expected. It lay at our feet, in a broad valley; a cluster of houses at the center, then fewer toward the river, which resembled a belt buckled with the clasp of the old bridge. The river was green, but, here and there, it shone golden. Wooded hills on the opposite bank were what made the river look green, and down at the foot of the hills, the fruit trees were full of white blossoms.

"You see, you see," I whispered to Jadwiga, as if I were taking credit for the beauty of this town that lay silent and calm at the bottom of a green valley, beside a large green river. I forgot about everything and stood there, also calm and silent. I closed my eyes: the air smelled of flowers. It was a brief moment, painful despite its bliss. When I opened my eyes, I saw Jadwiga's profile against the background of the green hills and the blooming white trees. I saw her flushed, hot face and the stains on her navy-blue school coat. "We'll leave the shoes in the bushes for the time being," I said, and continued upward along a path bulging with the roots of trees.

We sat down in a secluded place, on a fallen tree trunk. The grass was soft and lush. Sunshine filtered through the thick bushes. I took from my pocket the flat tin box I'd gotten from Gienek. There were still two cigarettes left. Jadwiga suggested that we save them for later, for some difficult hour, but I very much wanted to smoke.

The cigarette tasted awful. All I could think about was that it was the last one. I smoked slowly, postponing the moment of decision. Jadwiga took a fine-toothed comb out of her purse and started hunting for the lice that we had been unable to get rid of since our time at the camp. We were silent. I looked at her red cheeks, her chapped lips. I wanted to say something kind, but I didn't. I watched her searching for lice and finally shouted at her to stop it. Why bother? Who knew if any of this would work out? She put the comb in the pocket of her coat.

We moistened a handkerchief with dew and washed our faces, necks, and hands. Our hats and gloves lay on the grass. We were ready, and now we could no longer put off inventing new biographies and planning the rest of our journey. Jadwiga wrapped her arms around her knees and waited to hear what I would say. The veins on her hands were swollen. Her hands were the hands of an old woman, and my hands were like that, too. The bells that had been ringing loudly fell silent. The silence was now total, except for the birds that whistled from time to time in the bushes.

"The boys are coming back from the pasture now," said Jadwiga, and as she spoke I saw Gienek's sunburnt face. "I didn't know you were so . . . tough," he'd said, amused. I wasn't tough at all. I was scared to death, but now the memory of his words gave me courage.

"We've run away from a bombed factory," I said. "Our documents burned up during the air raid. We want to work for a farmer. We're terrified of bombs. The factory was in Wuppertal . . . or should we say Düsseldorf?"

"Stefan told me that the *Arbeitsamt* in Dortmund burned down. He thought we should keep that in mind."

"All right. We've escaped from Dortmund. If it's true that the *Arbeitsamt* was bombed, they won't be able to check our documents. It was a munitions factory, we spent six months there. We don't know its name, we're just two dumb country girls."

Our own experience made it easy for us to invent Barbara and Maria's pasts. We put them in the countryside, in a peasant family. Barbara had no parents, and Maria had been disowned by her father, a railroad worker who was tyrannized by his mean second wife—her evil stepmother. But that was only the beginning. What next? How would we shape the fate of these girls who had escaped from the factory camp in Dortmund? When and where would they go? How would they get there? And what about the town, the river, the wineries?

No, I definitely didn't want to think about leaving yet. I didn't want to give up this town, which had again stirred my hunger for beauty. In Waldwiesen I used to run to the garden early every morning to look at the delicate, pink peach blossoms. I had never before been so sensitive to the beauty of nature. Things I'd always taken for granted now moved me deeply, gave me that feeling of painful sweetness I'd experienced a moment ago when that view of the town suddenly emerged from behind a curve.

It was too beautiful to leave right away. We had until evening. And although this day no longer belonged to Jadwiga and Joanna, let it not be Barbara and Maria's day, either. Let it be a day of the nameless, of those not written down on any list, of those who were not registered and therefore did not exist.

"We'll decide what to do in the evening," I said. "Perhaps we won't go any further. Perhaps we'll stay here. How many miles have we traveled? Two hundred? Three hundred? Perhaps that's enough."

"But how?" Jadwiga grew frightened. "You said the farther away the better, and you wanted to go all the way south, down to the lake, close to the border."

I thought: Yes, I wanted to; I still want to. She was right. I was only toying with the thought of staying among these beautiful hills by the wide green river. It would have been so nice to stay there. Even the name of this town carried the fragrance of wild berries and of the forest. I liked towns with pleasant-sounding names, but I knew that at night we would continue on, all the way south, down to the lake, as Jadwiga-Barbara said. Because the farther away we went, the safer we'd be.

But just then I didn't want to think about the guards at strange train stations; the dim lobbies with their little ticket windows; the huge timetables from which we would randomly choose our destination and our time of departure; the moment when we would have to say where we were going, casually, our accents flawless, and then with gloved hands, the gloves that hid rough skin and fingers black from peeling tons of potatoes, pick up our tickets from the brass plate. Most of all, I didn't want to think about the stares of the other passengers on the train, which, with every mile would bring us closer to the birth of Barbara and Maria, to the moment when we would be asked our names and have to say them aloud, the moment from which there would be no turning back.

I didn't want to think about all that and so I said that we had until evening. It was as if we had given ourselves a leave, a vacation. The distressed grimace left Jadwiga's face; relief smoothed her features.

We hid the shoes in the bushes and returned to town down the same road we'd taken up the mountain. We walked briskly, smiling and quietly humming *"Everything passes; night turns to day,"* as we did when Marysia-Anna was with us.

The curve again afforded us a view of the river and the hills: a colorful postcard. The river, which in the morning had been green and empty, was now blue, with skiffs and rowboats floating down it.

This image of the town was obviously false. I had been thinking of it as empty, without human breath, without human speech. I had left out its inhabitants. But even while I gladly embraced this partial impression, I knew that it would soon be completed against my will, and that—in a familiar moment of weariness and sudden sadness, the sort of moment that usually comes at the end of the day—my enchantment would give way to hatred, and my happiness to despair.

But for the time being, those people thronging the streets, the same people we had seen in the morning on their way to church, didn't bother me at all. Now there were crowds of them. Slow and dignified, they strolled through the city on this beautiful day, and their speech was softer than it had been in the north, free of the harsh, threatening, guttural sounds that used to horrify us. The women wore no lipstick; their hair was carefully waved; they left behind trails of perfume. Their shoes were astonishing: polished like mirrors.

Jadwiga was thirsty. We looked for a refreshment stand, which would be safer than a café. But there was no kiosk on that busy street, only little tables with umbrellas. So we went deeper into the town, into the silent, empty side streets. A little old man in an old-fashioned coat was walking a dachshund on a leash; they disappeared inside the door of an old building. A woman with a baby in a stroller smiled at us as we passed. I told myself, "That means we must look decent." The stores were closed. Jadwiga kept whispering, "I don't want to look at anything. I just want to drink . . . to drink."

We came to a small plaza that led steeply down toward the river; we walked to the riverbank. Now the town with the castle hill reigning over it seemed to shrink; from where we stood, it looked like a cramped little town—its houses piled up, one on top of the other—pressed into a wall of greenery. Skiffs and rowboats still glided on the blue river, the same men and women continued their stately promenade along the embankment. And they still didn't bother me, I felt no fear. I was laughing inside, a low, cunning laugh: Look at us! We're strolling among you, strolling along your river, as if there were nothing to it. And in Waldwiesen, Klothilde was asking her husband: "Did they catch those Jews yet?" "Don't worry," Schulz was answering. "They'll catch them, all right. Have no fear."

I still felt no fear. This mood was lulling and therefore dangerous—but we were on vacation till evening. A boat had just docked at the marina. In addition to the horseshoe, I had thirty marks in my purse. It was enough for a ride, and for the rest of our journey. In front of us was a young woman with a three-year-old boy: "Look, Hansi, what a fast motorboat! Look, Hansi, what a pretty rowboat." The boy wore a sailor suit with gold buttons. Of course, the child was innocent—though he too probably said, "*unser Führer*" and "*Heil Hitler.*" In his mother's eyes there was a blissful, bovine calm. She noticed me watching her and seemed on the verge of chatting. She wasn't much older than I. She was bathed, all fresh for the holiday, fresh and clean. Damn it, damn it, damn it. We should have stayed away from this crowd.

I saw a flash of horror in the woman's eyes. I heard her scream. Calm, I thought, stay calm . . .

Jadwiga was on her knees, drinking water from the river. She was drinking like a thirsty animal.

I grabbed her hand; it was hot. "Hedwig," I said, using her German name, "are you ill? Get up, Hedwig, we're going home, you're still too weak . . . *Komm, Hedwig, komm.*"

The words came pouring out. Talk, keep talking, ward off all questions, convince them she's fainted, convince them she wasn't drinking.

I picked her up from the ground. I put my arm around her. "Let's go home." People cleared a path for us. "She just felt ill. Thank you, she's fine now, everything's fine." There were a few bursts of laughter, a few guarded, curious stares. This was the end of our journey, the end. In a moment, a cool, polite voice would say: "Papers, please."

"Please don't be angry."

"Quiet, not a word from you."

No one came near us. Luckily, they couldn't imagine it, they just couldn't believe she had been drinking river water, in broad daylight, on this festive day. No, she simply fainted: she just felt ill.

"Don't be angry."

"I'm not. We'll go to a café. You need something to drink."

"I don't want to go to a café. I'm scared. I want to sleep."

"There's a forest on the other side of the river. We'll get some sleep there. Everything will pass."

"Is anyone following us?"

"No."

"What will you do if I die on the way?"

"Don't be an idiot. You'll get some sleep, you'll get well."

The first kiosk we found was by the entrance to the bridge. Jadwiga drank two bottles of beer. There was no seltzer. The woman selling the drinks looked at us, friendly, but a little too curious. We walked away, quickly.

*

We lay in the tall grass, among blossoming cherry trees. The smell was wonderful. We could see the river through the branches of the trees, and we could hear laughter and snatches of conversation coming from the footpath. Crickets were chirping, and we heard the sound of a scythe being sharpened. It was high noon. The sun was at its zenith.

Jadwiga slept. She had fallen asleep immediately. She was breathing heavily. Her face was swollen. She should have been in a hospital. She was very ill. But she had to get well because there was no other way. "She will get well, she will get well," I kept repeating. I didn't really believe in magic spells, but I was resorting to them now. We should have run away as soon as Anna got back the letter she had written to Paulina, with the notation *"zur Zeit Gestapo"* . . . This Anna, she's a Jew, *eine Jüdin*" . . . We will go all the way south, the lake is called the Bodensee, my name is Maria Walkowska, and Jadwiga is now . . .

I was awakened by the rustle of a light spring rain. I jumped up and covered our hats with my coat. Jadwiga was no longer asleep. She was sitting with her back toward me.

I said, "Are you feeling better?"

"Better," she said. "That beer helped me. I'm eating the meat."

"What are you talking about? What meat?"

"Stefan gave me a tin of meat for the trip. I had it in my coat pocket. I didn't tell you because you would have yelled at me. I made a hole in the can with a sharp rock. I'm getting the meat out with a stick. It's salty, but it's good."

"Throw it away! Right now! A week of fasting and fever—and now meat on an empty stomach? Throw it away. Next thing, you'll be drinking water from the river again."

"I won't throw it away. That would be a waste. And it's good meat. Have some."

"We'll go and have a real meal, but throw that awful stuff away."

I grabbed the can from her hand and threw it into the bushes.

"Get up. It's raining. We're going back to town."

We went back across the bridge, but instead of going toward the center, we walked in the opposite direction. It was drizzling, the river was gray, the riverbank was empty. On the outskirts of the city, I thought, we might find a little place to eat. We would relax a bit, then return to town, walk around until the evening, and then board a train heading south. The nap on the grass had done me good, and the fact that Jadwiga was recovering made me feel even better. I just had to keep my mind off the next day—the thought of tomorrow felt heavy inside me, I couldn't allow it to weigh me down. I had to concentrate on the present, not think about what was coming next.

We pushed open a gate with an elaborate door-knocker and entered a restaurant in a spacious one-story building covered thickly with vines. In the dim interior, under a carved wooden ceiling, slim, graceful waitresses bustled back and forth in black dresses and microscopic white aprons. The room was full. Glasses of red wine glowed on the tables; fragrant smoke hung in the air. It was not a country tavern but rather an elegant restaurant disguised by a rustic exterior.

The only free table, bigger than the rest, was in the center of the room, and that was where we sat. I took off my wet coat, draped it casually over my shoulders, and looked around. The place was packed with soldiers, red-faced and laughing boisterously. A waitress materialized in front of us, stylishly black-and-white. I looked at her white, well-groomed hands, and hid mine under my coat.

"Meat, please."

It was Jadwiga speaking, Jadwiga, who had been silent during the entire journey, who had pretended not to hear, to be asleep, who had been afraid to utter a single word in their language. And now, she suddenly spoke up—to order meat, which was strictly rationed. The only thing on her mind was that she had to eat something.

"What kind of meat would you like?"

The waitress's voice was extremely polite, with only a trace of irony.

"What would you recommend?" I gave Jadwiga a warning look, opened my purse, and first calmly, then impatiently, searched for the ration coupons.

"My goodness! We left our coupons at home."

The white, well-groomed hands made a helpless gesture. A quick gaze from Jadwiga said: But I must.

"In that case we'll have something that doesn't require coupons."

"Potato salad?"

She did not hide the contempt in her smile.

"Yes, please. Two portions."

At the sight of the potatoes with onions, Jadwiga could barely control her eagerness or her shaking hands. The first real meal in ten days! We would have liked one more portion, but we were afraid to show how hungry we were.

We paid the waitress, whose scorn for us was now obvious, and left the room. At the same moment, a man in a military uniform jumped up from his table and followed us. Perhaps he just needed some fresh air; or perhaps . . .

We walked slowly, stopped, buttoned our coats.

"Remember, we escaped from Dortmund," I whispered to Jadwiga.

The military man was watching us. We stood only a few yards from him.

"And now we really must be getting home," I said loudly. But we didn't hurry. We walked calmly away.

Darkness fell quickly, and now, in the evening, the town looked quite different than it had in the morning. It looked like an ordinary town on a cloudy, rainy day. Neon signs and shop windows gleamed. People entered and left houses, restaurants, cafés. Above the entrance to a movie theater glowed the huge face of the actress Christine Soderbaum.

We walked aimlessly this way and that; our growing fatigue kept bringing us back to the river, where we could rest. It was quiet and calm by the river. We stood there, talking every now and then, but not about anything important. Behind us rose the castle hill—our make-believe home in this town—with Jadwiga's shoes hidden in its bushes.

A new downpour drove us into an ice cream parlor (we ate raspberry ice cream, sweet as candy) and there I saw our faces in a mirror. We still had not aroused any suspicion, but when I looked at those girls in the mirror, I told myself: We have to resume our journey right away and travel all night on the train, so that in the morning we will be near the lake, near the border.

A cheerful-looking young man asked, "What are you doing this evening? Shall we go see a movie?"

I grabbed Jadwiga, and we went out into the street. Water was streaming down the sidewalks. People were running with their shoulders hunched, running to their dry, warm homes, to their lamps above their tables, to their books in their bookcases.

Now came that moment at the end of the day, that difficult moment we were not allowed to succumb to. More and more slowly, more and more sluggishly, we walked toward the train station. Look, I said to myself, this really is a beautiful city, even now, in the rain and darkness, it is a prettier town than most. But my words were hollow, and all I felt was exhaustion. Only when we got to the square in front of the station did Jadwiga realize where we were headed.

"And my shoes?" she asked with such fear and horror that I stopped, confused. Should we go back to the castle hill or leave right away? I thought about the dim station lobby and imagined myself in front of the timetable, squinting, without my glasses, then walking up to the ticket office.

"Let's go back to the hill," I said. We started up the same road we'd taken in the morning and, as if to prove that we'd made the right decision, the rain suddenly stopped, and the smell of acacias filled the air.

We were climbing, Jadwiga in front of me: thin,

stooped, wobbling on the heels of her oversized shoes. She looked like an old woman. With every uphill curve of the road, the town receded farther and farther away, and fell into the fog and the darkness. The evening and the fog made the hill seem different. We hardly recognized it and now had trouble finding the place where Jadwiga had hidden her shoes.

I kept telling her to leave them. What do you need them for? But she wouldn't give them up. She explained in a breathless voice that she had to find them, she couldn't leave them lying in the bushes. She talked about them the way one talks about a child. She asked me to close my eyes, as I had in the forest when we'd gotten lost, when Marysia-Anna was still with us.

I agreed. I stopped, closed my eyes, and reimagined the way to the bushes. The grass was wet. The shoes, when I found them, were slimy and soaked through. There was nothing to wrap them in, because the newspaper fell apart in our fingers like a spider web. But Jadwiga didn't care. She cradled the shoes like a puppy under her coat and carried them like that.

We had already climbed quite high and still hadn't found a good place to lie down. I sat on a bench. I didn't feel like going on, and I immediately fell into a shallow sleep. I knew that I was sleeping, I knew my mouth was open, and I also knew that this was bad, that it was bad I no longer wanted to walk and look for a place to lie down. My loss of desire was the worst possible thing. And the most dangerous. But I couldn't help it, and I couldn't wake up.

I heard Jadwiga's voice saying, "Joanna, Joanna, wake up, don't sleep." Her voice was full of fear because I'd fallen asleep so suddenly and with my mouth gaping. At last she grabbed my arm. I opened my eyes and saw a strange face leaning over me. It was Jadwiga's face, streaming with tears. "Don't start bawling," I said.

"I'm not bawling. It's the rain."

The brief, shallow nap had made me feel a lot stronger. I jumped up from the bench and soon found a good place to sleep, underneath a canopy of thick branches. I told Jadwiga to take her coat off, and did the same myself. We used her coat to cover our hats, and mine to make a tent wide enough for both of us.

I got up again and searched for the lights of the town below. They had disappeared in the fog. The birds, too, were gone, driven away by the rain, which was once again falling in heavy sheets, whipped by the wind.

*

Sunlight woke me. I immediately checked our hats. They were still dry, the coat had protected them from the rain. I put my straw hat on and took a mirror out of my purse. I looked at myself for a moment. Brown suited me; the bunches of flowers pinned to the rim of my hat were fresh and cheerful. *"Zweimal bitte, dritte Klasse,"* I said and smiled at the mirror. Then I took off my hat, washed my face with wet leaves, and woke Jadwiga.

I said, "Barbara, get up!" For the first time I used her new name, her third one, and from that moment on she was Barbara. Jadwiga ceased to exist. Joanna ceased to exist, too; her place was taken by Maria. We adopted and discarded names, invented and altered biographies, created new characters and had absolute power over them.

A pale, rain-washed sun shone over the town. I didn't stop at the curves, didn't look down at the hills and the river, even though they were probably beautiful in the morning sun. I was no longer interested in this town.

"*Zweimal Karlsruhe, dritte Klasse,*" I said, and smiled.

"*Zweimal Kahsruh?*" asked the clerk. Later, the baker would tell me that only foreigners pronounced each syllable separately, pretentiously: *Karls* and *ruhe*, foreigners and—once upon a time—Jews, before the Führer sent them to their maker. ("What in the world are you talking about?" the baker's wife exclaimed in alarm. "He sent them to America.") Everyone else pronounced it in the local dialect: Kahsruh.

I immediately realized my mistake. The clerk's gaze lingered briefly on my hat brim, then moved down to my leather gloves. "Here you are."

At that early hour the train was still empty. Automatically, without having to speak, we did what we'd done on our previous train rides: Barbara covered herself with her coat and pretended to be asleep. Opposite her, I sat erect, with my hands on my knees, looking out the window. I heard voices on the platform. "*Hah-yo, hah-yo, gesta, hah-yo . . .*" "*Hah-yo*" sounded like a farmer cheerfully calling his cows, but "*gesta*" made me shiver—Gestapo? No, *gestern*, "yesterday," in dialect. "Yesterday it rained so hard."

In three hours we would be in Karlsruhe. What kind

of city would it be? Would it fulfill the promise contained in its name, the promise of calm, of peace? *Ruhe, Ruhe.* "*Du bist die Ruh*' . . ." That was why we had chosen this town out of all the towns between here and the lake, because its name promised peace, calm.

What would Marysia-Anna say if she were here with us? Would she like the name? Anna didn't like the picturesque, musical name, Iserlohn. She preferred the crisp-sounding Arnsberg. But I was repelled by the tightly clumped consonants "rns." We were standing under a road sign, on a dark night. Listen: *Iserlohn* . . . it sounds like meadows. What happened to Anna? Where did she escape to? First, there were six of us, then three, now there were two . . .

Quietly, gently, with a slight lurch, the train started moving. I felt a knot in my stomach and a lump in my throat, as always. *Ruhe, Ruhe.* Peace.

An elderly woman entered the compartment. She had white hair, and wore a velvet ribbon around her neck, and a ring on her finger. Was it an old family ring or was it a gift from her son on the Eastern Front? Ridiculous. Don't think like that, smile back, but distantly, coolly: conversations are undesirable.

Barbara's eye peering out from under the coat sent me a signal: I'm not asleep, I'm watching, I can see and hear everything, and I'm ready at any moment.

The woman on the night train had been younger, but also dressed in black. Many women were wearing black these days. There were many expensive rings on women's fingers, many expensive fur coats . . . our brave soldiers . . . in the newspapers, long lists of those who had "fallen for the Führer and the Fatherland . . ."

"Good day," the woman said. Barbara's watchful eye gazed out from under a sleeve. The woman with the velvet ribbon around her neck said I reminded her of her daughter. I smiled. Her daughter had similar hair, ash blond, and the same Nordic looks. Tall, fair-skinned, and slender. In the camp, I was as thin as a stick; now, after Klothilde's diet, I was slender and Nordic. Her daughter was supposed to come home soon on vacation. She missed her a lot. That was why she was staring at me. A mother's heart. Perhaps it was her son who pulled the ring off the finger of my dying mother?

Nonsense. My mother, Leokadia Walkowska, née Wiecek, died giving birth to me. After her death, my father started drinking, and married Waclawa Piekarska. My father drank, my stepmother beat me, I had a bad childhood, a bad adolescence. I volunteered for hard labor rather than stay at home: me, Maria Walkowska. What was the mother of a daughter who looked like me asking? I didn't hear. I was too busy thinking about the family of the alcoholic railroad worker. Barbara signaled with her eye: Be careful. Barbara had heard what the old hag was asking. Hag? That was wrong. She was my fellow countrywoman. I shouldn't call her a hag. I thought: You forgot. You're not Maria Walkowska yet. You are a German girl—*ein deutsches Mädchen*.

The old lady asked what was wrong with my finger.

I said I had hurt myself at the factory. "Oh, you work in a factory? In a munitions plant?"

"Yes, yes," I said, and I smiled. In fact, my finger was hurt from peeling too many potatoes in Klothilde Schulz's kitchen. "Yes, yes, in a munitions plant." She was delighted. We were both delighted. Our brave German girls! "Before she left for the East, my daughter also worked in a munitions plant." Our conversation had gone a little too far. I looked out the window: green and more green, a pretty country of fertile earth, green landscapes, a beautiful land, a brave land. *Heil, heil.*

"Excuse me?" She asked if I would let her fix my bandage. The gauze had become untied. She wanted to do at least that much for the brave young girl who resembled her daughter. The dressing was dirty, its ends were hanging pitifully. When I'd escaped, I'd remembered to bandage the brave German girl's finger, because nowadays, in brave German households, potatoes were peeled by savage foreigners from the East, but yesterday, on the castle hill, I forgot to put on a fresh dressing, neatly tied. What would the German mother think if she saw my blackened finger, cut by the paring knife?

"Oh, no thank you. It's not necessary. I can manage." But my finger was already in her leathery hand. Her ring sparkled . . .

"It hurts, it hurts, please don't untie it all the way."

Oh, she didn't mean to hurt me, she apologized. No, no, *vielen Dank*, I'm very grateful, and a smile. But that was far enough. I turned my head, looked out the window, and shut my eyes. Sleep. *Ein deutsches Mädchen* was sleeping, Maria Walkowska was ready and watchful, and I still felt the lump in my throat.

*

Ruhe? The city whose name promised serenity greeted us with ominous banners: countless swastikas fluttered above the station square. This treacherous city was celebrating some sinister holiday. We should have left immediately, but we walked defiantly through the square, the black twisted crosses above our heads. We walked toward the street, leaving the station behind. Not a word had been spoken, but we already knew: we would not see the lake.

The decision was made unexpectedly, silently, because of our faces. In the bright light of the morning, our faces no longer looked right for travel. Our fear, too, was unexpected: the proximity of the border, which had previously lured us on, now frightened us away. Near the border they would be checking more carefully, watching more closely, more suspiciously. How could I not have thought of this before? Before it was just the lake, the lake . . . as if we could simply swim across it. What a fool I had been!

"It was a stupid plan," I said aloud. "Stupid and dangerous."

We were sitting on a bench. Before us was a street, full of morning traffic. We watched cars and streetcars. A wave of girls came down the street, carrying satchels. Their long, neatly braided hair flowed down their backs. There must have been a girls' school nearby. We followed them with our vacant stares. They were happy and bright and kept coming, wave after wave.

Listlessness and lethargy overwhelmed us. We had to get up and let ourselves get caught; it would be better to get caught than to turn ourselves in. The best place would be on the outskirts, or in a nearby small town, not in the city itself. But we stayed on the bench. The morning had progressed, the sun appeared from behind the clouds, the streetcars clanged.

The waves of girls had passed. Now an elderly woman walked by, and as she passed us, she stopped, as if she were wondering whether to approach us and say something. But she turned away and walked on, with a bunch of yellow jonquils in her hand. She had a beautiful face and heavy, beautiful eyes; around her shoulders she wore a patterned shawl. I hadn't seen women like that here before—was she an artist, an actress? I memorized her face. I remember exactly the entire episode on the bench across the square from the sinister banners: the waves of girls, the yellow jonquils, our languor.

A streetcar took us to a distant suburb and stopped at a circular plaza. I liked that huge plaza, filled with trees. The tops of the trees looked like domes. On the right, behind the trees, stood a long gray stone building that looked like a convent. We were the only ones getting off at this stop. It was almost noon. The sun was very warm.

"We'll let ourselves get caught here," I said.

"By whom?" asked Barbara. "There's no one around."

Just at that moment, a policeman emerged from under the trees, walking unhurriedly; gravel crunched under his feet. We started toward him, talking clearly and loudly in Polish about our craving for potatoes, for noodles, for food,

food. That was the only subject that occurred to us. The policeman passed and disappeared under the trees, but after a while he again emerged nearby; the plaza was clearly his beat. For a long time we circled him, waiting in vain for the words: "Papers, please." He was silent. So we approached him. "*Essen. Pole.*"

He led us toward the gray building that looked like a convent: the sign said POLIZEI. The policeman opened the old wooden gate for us, then closed it. I can see all this, as if on film, especially the old gate opening and closing; perhaps it once did lead to a convent. I can also recall the darkness that then surrounded us. In that darkness we walked upstairs, into a large room full of policemen, all laughing raucously.

When they saw us they fell silent.

The next hour would bring us to the edge of the abyss: an interrogation, a battle of wits with a woman interpreter who didn't believe us.

"Unheard of!" she kept exclaiming. "That's a lie, the girl's lying."

She was smart and treacherous; she purposely mistranslated what we said, she wanted us to lose. And we lost. A tall, thin policeman with a hawklike face announced: "I'm calling the Gestapo."

He dialed the number, and at that very moment, the station commander opened the door. Sheer chance, the perfect concurrence of two events. The policeman put down the receiver.

"There's something wrong here," he said, "a strange case. I'm calling the Gestapo."

The commander, a short, fat man, approached us, looked us over, walked away, came back, and finally ordered, "Call the *Arbeitsamt*."

Once more the hawkfaced policeman reached for the receiver.

*

As we rode the streetcar back into town, I asked myself if I hadn't been too quick to suspect this town of betrayal and deceit. We were riding, as we had once before, up north, with a clerk from the *Arbeitsamt* who had been summoned to pick us up. "Village, milk cow, no factory." He nodded yes, and glanced at my hat, which I was holding in my hand. He didn't ask any questions. It had been the smart, treacherous interpreter who kept harping on the hat; it intrigued her. Once, twice, three times she demanded, "And the hat—who'd you steal it from? Did you wear a hat like that at home?" It was hard to tell why it so fascinated her. Her abrupt and repeated demands for the name of the factory were more understandable.

"So, what was the name of that factory in Dortmund?"

"I already said: Gembha."

"Don't pretend you don't know that GmbH is the acronym for 'limited.' 'Gembha' is *not* the *name* of a factory. Take my advice. Try to remember the name of that factory. And don't lie. You're lying."

"But those were the letters, G-m-B-H. Gembha . . . or something . . ."

"She's a sly one, sly . . ."

"Klarissa," the hawk-face kept saying to her, "That's enough, Klarissa, there's no point, I'll call the Gestapo, the Gestapo will make her talk . . ."

At the *Arbeitsamt*, I slid my hat under my coat and repeated: Village, cow, milk.

"*Ja, ja*, cow, milk," the clerk said impatiently. "You two will work in the same village, for different farmers. The *Bauernführer*—the village mayor—is picking you up in his car."

*

Later she used to say: The place where everything almost ended. She meant the long, gray stone building on the circular plaza planted with trees.

But why that place? After all, there were other places equally, if not more deserving of that description. And yet, thirty years later, it was that place she went to see, only that one place.

This was a real village: small houses along a carriage road that gradually descended and trailed off into the forest; in the yards, heaps of manure neatly tamped down with a spade; meadows and fields all around; in the center of the village, a church, a spreading lime tree, the town hall, and a creamery; under the lime tree, a bench; on the church steeple, a rooster, a weathervane turned by the wind; on the road, a cart passing, pulled by cows, not horses—the *Bauernführer* and the blacksmith were the only ones who owned horses, everyone else used cows to work the fields. It was a real village, of not very prosperous peasants. All it lacked were orchards: apple trees, pear trees, plum trees grew here and there in the fields or by the country roads. And soft wooded hills rose on the horizon.

The car stopped under the lime tree. A skinny farmer's wife with a goiter on her neck and three small children in tow ran down the wooden stairs of the house at the back of the yard. A farmer emerged from the cow barn and stuck his pitchfork into the manure hill. He raised his arm. *Heil Hitler*.

"This is your Pole." The *Bauernführer* pointed to Barbara.

They thanked him profusely: "Many thanks, Fridolin, many thanks, *a feines Mädele*—a nice girl."

"*Mädele*, not *Mädchen*—the people around here talk like Jews," laughed Zygmunt, the Pole who worked at the blacksmith's shop. "And they even look like Jews. Dark and sickly—you'd think you were in Palestine."

Three houses down, behind the counter inside the little shop, stood fat, redheaded Hermina in her starched apron. The baker came up from his bakery in the cellar, and he was exactly as Zygmunt described: dark and short. He skipped the part about Hitler, mumbled *guten Tag*, and Hermina began chattering away: How wonderful that they finally got someone to work. It was so difficult for them. They weren't young. What's your name? Maria. So that's our Maria, *a feines Mädele* . . .

In the evening, in my spacious attic room, I wrote, "Will I find peace here? Peace. I yearn for peace." Out of habit, I hid the sheet of paper under the mattress, where it stayed, blank, except for that one line of fine handwriting at the top. In contrast to the time when I'd been Joanna, now I had no desire to write. Maria was gaining on me. That first night I had a dream about a clearing in a forest in which there was a little wooden house, locked and bolted, uninhabited, surrounded by a low, wooden fence. The next Sunday, Barbara and I went to the woods for a walk and

there, suddenly, I saw the house from my dream. We took
this as a good omen.

*

Outside the window of the dark little kitchen was a small,
neglected farmyard. There were two cows in the barn. The
room adjoining the kitchen was just big enough for two
beds. In the front, beside the store, was the "good room,"
a sacred place, which was always locked, and inside stood
Hermina's pride, a glass-fronted cabinet. She would not let
me clean that room and insisted on dusting the bric-a-brac
and the furniture herself. They received guests there on
special occasions—only twice during my stay. But every
Sunday, Hermina sat there by the window, in her Sunday
dress and Sunday apron, holding an open book, but not
reading, hidden behind a partly drawn curtain, observing
the people who strolled down the road.

From her conversations in the store and her Sundays
by the window, she knew everything that happened in the
village. She left the store only during the harvest and the
potato-digging season; she liked to point out that she came
from a city. People regarded her with respect, but not without irony, the woman hidden behind her curtain, the wife
of the baker who liked jokes, women, and politics. He was
an alcoholic. He'd paid for a drunken rant in a tavern with
a stay in a camp—and that was even before the war. On
one of my very first days there, as the cows pulled our cart
out to the field, he told me about it, in the primitive German
he thought a foreigner would understand. "Maria, you are

Pole, you know, I say Hitler no good, and I in camp one year."

He had spent a year in Dachau; Hermina had bought his freedom with sacks of flour. After he came back, people were contemptuous of him and avoided him. He was an impulsive, hot-tempered man. He no longer went to the tavern and now delivered his convoluted drunken monologues in the kitchen. "He's preaching again," Hermina would complain and hurriedly shut the windows.

Toward the end, he changed. He no longer whispered to me, "Hitler no good." Instead he exclaimed, "We'll show you yet!" as if, despite his own convictions, he could not accept the thought of ultimate defeat.

*

In this small village at the foot of the gentle hills everything was different than it had been up north: the landscape, the people, their language. And we were different. The experience and knowledge we'd gained from working for the wealthy farmers in Waldwiesen had given us confidence and peace of mind. Barbara had recovered, and for the first time she wasn't worried about her black hair and dark eyes: many of the villagers had similar eyes and hair, and also, down here, it was commonly believed that Poles were dark.

"Most Poles are brunettes," said the baker, and he wasn't the only one who said it. In the eyes of the villagers, Barbara was a perfect specimen of Polish womanhood. Freed from anxiety about her dark looks and from the harassments of her former German mistress, she no longer resembled either Elzbieta or Jadwiga. She came back to life. The farmer's wife took every occasion to tell her children about the greatness of the Führer, the farmer himself wore the party badge, but they treated their Polish girl decently; they had waited a long time for a farmhand from the East. Barbara came back to life, grew strong and energetic. We were no longer silent with each other. Now I often said to her: "This time *you* decide."

Maria was different, too. She virtually took on a life of her own; sometimes (not too often!) she actually dominated me. For example, when I was alone with Barbara, I would suddenly find myself talking like a peasant, like the person I was pretending to be. Or riding in the cart out to the field, I would feel a blissful calm, and it would occur to me that later I could live just like this: simply and peacefully, without all the things I used to need, in a world defined by fields, meadows, rakes, cows . . .

I didn't like Maria gaining on me, even though I was working so hard to become her.

Less and less often we used the word "if"; more and more often we simply said "when," and wondered whether we would ever be like we used to be.

Our fear of being found out or recognized had not gone away. It had only dug itself in deeper and was taking a little nap. Sometimes this fear would awaken suddenly and mistake a salesman for a secret policeman—like the cattle merchant who spoke to the baker behind closed doors. It would awaken suddenly and then fall back asleep. The more time passed, the deeper it slept. But even toward the end, after the British occupied the Ruhr Valley, when our fear should have disappeared completely—even then remnants of it still remained within us. They lingered in us until the very end, until that day—still far off—when two armored cars from General de Gaulle's army drove through the village, and Gottfried, the local party leader, climbed onto the roof of his house and jammed a flagpole into a crevice between the roof tiles—a flagpole with a white sheet attached.

*

Piotr was the first to come see us. He came from Waldbach when he heard that two Polish girls had arrived, and from then on he came every Sunday until the bombs fell on the sawmill.

He had the rolling gait of a sailor, but he was a mason from Warsaw. He wore a black suit, an old-fashioned vest and a hat; he was a little formal, melancholy, soft-spoken and gentle. He was forty, and an orphan. Later we felt badly that we hadn't told him the truth. He often said that he felt we were like family. He would bring us small gifts, things you could buy without ration coupons: colorful combs, little mirrors, bunches of artificial violets. We never told him the truth.

Piotr brought Olek, and Olek's wife, and Rudolf, a Pole from France: they all worked in the sawmill.

We would sit at Barbara's on a broken sofa, in her tiny room with its view of the lime tree and the church with the rooster, or sometimes in the clearing in the forest, near the little hunter's cabin I had dreamed about before I saw it. Sometimes we read poems from a book Olek had brought from Poland. From the upper village came delicate fifteen-year-old Helenka. And once a month Genowefa would come from the labor camp near the town. They were hungry in the camp. She came to get the ration coupons for bread and sugar that I stole from Hermina's store.

Olek was no longer in Waldbach when the bombs hit the sawmill. He had been sick and had managed to get a permit to return to Poland. Six bombs fell at noon. Piotr didn't want to go down to the bomb shelter. Along with Rudolf, he stood outside the mill, looking up at the sky. I was sweeping the farmyard when the windowpanes in the village began to shake.

Rudolf was seriously injured and taken to a field hospital. We searched for him in vain. Someone told us Piotr's last words: "To the shelter? To be buried under the rubble with the Germans?"

The funeral was held the next evening. The priest never finished his prayer; the planes roared overhead, circling low. We hid between the tombstones. It was dark and close, Helenka cried from fear.

*

The front line drew near, then stopped on the other side of the Rhine, in Alsace. I can see, as if it happened yesterday, Maria on her way to Luisa Hess to get vodka for the baker. She was dragging her feet in her clogs. She had not finished the milking. Dressed for the stable, she wore a smock and a kerchief pulled down on her forehead. She was shuffling to the neighbors who brewed vodka and apple wine. In those days, the baker was drinking heavily.

Luisa Hess, skinny and dark, looked like an Italian,

or a Spaniard or a Gypsy, anything but a German. She went down to the basement to get the vodka, and Maria, in her stable clothes, stood (I see it as if it were yesterday) by the door.

She was not alone in the room. At the table, drinking wine, were scientists from a city that had been destroyed in a bombing raid. They were living in the new, as yet unused school building, though no one knew exactly what they were doing there. It was rumored that they were working on the new weapon that the Führer had promised the nation; people feared that their presence would attract bombs to the village.

There were four of them: an ascetic-looking professor and three assistants. Maria could see them from the corner of her eye, but she didn't want to look at them and was ignoring their presence. The school building was near the bakery, so she knew these four, with their Master Race manners, their gazes that went straight through her, as if she didn't exist. She wasn't looking at the table, but rather, straight ahead at the grand piano on which a scrawny, pasty-faced assistant was playing a waltz. She was reluctant to look even at the piano, but she was determined not to look at the men at the table, so she had little choice. Meanwhile, Luisa lingered in the cellar, as if to spite her. The setting sun was blindingly bright, and Maria stood there lit by the red sun shining through the window.

"A primitive race." The professor was speaking. From the corner of her eye she watched his ascetic face. "Primitive, lazy, dirty. They live in filth." After a moment he added,

"She's probably never seen anyone play a piano. Perhaps you'd like to explain it to her, Hans?"

The pasty-faced young man laughed. "Come here, look. All you have to do is press this key with your finger. Want to try?"

She thought: Don't do anything stupid, don't be an idiot, but even so, she walked on toward the piano. The pale Hans played one key, then another, and again asked if she wanted to try. She reached out her hand. The high C sounded like a moan, the piano was out of tune. Behind her, someone laughed, and Hans asked, "Do you like it? *Schön?* Isn't it pretty?" She said, "*Schön,*" and, suddenly happy, repeated: *Schön, schön,* pretty, pretty.

At that moment something shifted inside her, something moved.

"A primitive race," repeated the professor. She laughed out loud, and, laughing, she struck one key after another, even as, frightened and breathless, she said to herself: "Stop, don't do it, there's still time."

From the table came laughter. Now there were two sorts of laughter in the room: theirs and hers.

With her elbow, she pushed away the pale Hans. She sat down, and played an A major chord. She was no longer laughing. Her heart was pounding dully. She began Chopin's famous Polonaise. After eight bars, she stopped. Her hands were shaking. She had to hide them in the pockets of her smock. The room was silent. She didn't look at the men at the table. Luisa ran up to her, exclaiming something, asking something; she looked amazed.

Maria smiled at her—she liked the dark, cheerful Luisa Hess—then took the bottle of vodka and left, shuffling loudly in her clogs.

Barbara paled when I told her what had happened. For a split second her face took on its old pained expression. All that night I didn't sleep. What would I say? How would I explain it? I remembered the baker's suspicion when he caught me reading a newspaper. "You're lying to us, you're pretending . . . What's the meaning of this?"

I had explained to him then that I was trying to read German, trying to put letters together and figure out the words. He believed me. What would he say now? And what would I say? Near dawn, as I lay awake, deep in thought, I heard the distant, hollow rumbling from the front that had been silent for several weeks.

That night the offensive began.

In the morning I told Hermina and the baker the doleful story of my fiancé who had played the organ at our church. He was the one who had taught me how to play the piano. I loved him deeply, but he had left me for someone else.

Hermina later told the whole story in the shop. "Our Maria had a fiancé who played the organ at the church," she would say. There was a note of pride in her voice.

*

They were near. They had crossed the Rhine. The sky glowed, and the sounds of the front came to us, rumbling and hollow. All day long we could hear the dry rattling of guns on the planes; the planes dived so low over the fields we could see the pilots' faces. Once, Barbara came running; she was pale and sweating, covered with dirt churned up by the bullets; a fragment of shrapnel had hit her in the leg. Again we thought, let us survive—but now we were talking about the bombs and the rattling guns.

German soldiers arrived that night. In the yard in front of the blacksmith's, steam rose from a field kitchen. Cars camouflaged with branches were parked under the chestnut trees. Two soldiers led Sergei, the gardener's helper, out of the village. I saw him being led away; all the blood had left his face. Apparently he had said something. Nobody ever saw him again. After a few days the *Wehrmacht* troops left the village.

"We are simple, decent people," Hermina kept saying. "We haven't hurt anyone. We have nothing to fear. They won't take revenge on the innocent. They won't let us starve to death." Once or twice she milked the cows herself.

A few bombs landed on the road, on the fields. A rock torn loose by the force of the explosion crashed onto the roof of the baker's house. Here and there, roof tiles were blown off—but that was all.

The night that turned out to be the last, Barbara stayed with me. The front was a mile or two away, the French were already in Waldbach. Just before dawn the shooting stopped, the explosions stopped. All was silent.

We climbed out of the cellar and left the house. In the pale dawn we could smell the fresh earth. A quiet murmur came from the woods; a huge plane appeared above the trees and glided through the brightening sky in a slow, easy loop. It circled the meadows, then disappeared behind the trees, then came back and circled again.

"This is it," I said to Barbara and watched this peaceful, quiet flight with an ache in my throat.

The two armored cars arrived at ten in the morning. It was the first Sunday of April 1945, a beautiful, clear, sunny day. They drove slowly from the upper part of the village to the lower. The white sheet fluttered on Gottfried's roof. I stood and waited. So that's how this moment looks: two armored cars on an empty country road. I felt nothing, only that pain in my throat.

It wasn't until the vehicles had rolled by that I felt overcome with joy. But I was still afraid to shout the full truth out loud. I shouted, "*Vive la France! Nous sommes Polonais!*" And the soldiers answered, "*Vive la Pologne!*" The tanks drove on without stopping, and disappeared beyond the bend in the road that entered the woods.

No one else came until evening. The sheet disappeared from Gottfried's roof, the village was the same as always. Nothing seemed to have changed.

It was already dark when a tank arrived and stopped for the night under the lime tree. Barbara saw it from the window of her room. She ran out, tore off a branch of jasmine, and gave it to the French soldiers.

We left early the next morning.

Hermina looked with astonishment at an old margarine box bound with a piece of the string farmers used to tie up sheafs of wheat—all my worldly possessions were inside. Under my arm, I clutched my purse with my documents and my half a horseshoe.

"What? You're leaving? Now, when there's so much work to do in the fields?"

She couldn't understand it. Was I unhappy with them? She had thought I would wait at least till the harvest. The baker was angry and silent.

Barbara was waiting under the lime tree, also with a box in her hand. We walked to the main highway that led to the city. Crowds of foreigners were already on the move, shouting happily to one another in different languages and raising their voices in one great song.

They returned. They returned and arrived in the city where their father was now living. They returned together, just as they had left together. They had left in darkness and they returned in darkness. Then it had been dusk, now the night was ending, and soon it would be dawn.

Oh, don't get melodramatic. What's the matter with you? They left at dusk because of the danger and returned at dawn because that was when their train arrived. Please, no symbols, no sentimentality.

Oh, but anything and everything is allowed at a moment like that, at such an exceptional moment; at such a moment, melodrama is not melodramatic, and even tears are permissible. But that was the hard part—she was still unable to cry.

During that whole time, she'd cried only once, when Jadwiga wrote to her: *Go without me. You'll be with Father, I'll be with Mother.* And even when Martine, from the UNRRA, told her to sit down, and she thought she was telling her to sit down because the news was bad, she just sat down obediently in the former officer's room that was now her room (the former SS quarters were now the UNRRA camp for displaced persons); and even when, after a brief silence, Martine said in a trembling voice, in French, "Your father is alive, your father has survived"—not even then did she cry. Maria turned pale, but Martine was the one with tears in her eyes.

The same thing happened shortly afterward—the messages came almost simultaneously, one after the other, one good, the other bad, both after long months of waiting—when she tore open the envelope and read the name, Marian, and another, unfamiliar name, Majdanek. She was standing by the window. Outside were the pines of the former SS forest. Mme. Durand, the secretary of the refugee camp, was walking under the pines, and when she saw her, waved cheerfully. Majdanek. She had never heard that name before. She knew: Auschwitz, Treblinka, Belzec. She knew: Bergen-Belsen, Mauthausen, but not Majdanek. She had never heard of Majdanek.

The day was about to break. Soon they could go out. They were sitting in the waiting room of the station in the city where Father now lived; he'd been repatriated from the Eastern regions to the lands acquired in the West—the Wild West, people called it.

They had been warned that it was dangerous to walk around the city at night, so they sat with everyone else in the waiting room. "Those two have come from far away," people whispered. "Maybe from a camp, maybe they're

Jewish. Many Jews are coming back these days. And they said they'd never . . ."

The day was beginning to break. Soon she would go out and look for Lakowa Street, and Barbara would stay with their two suitcases, which contained warm UNRRA blankets, warm UNRRA sweaters and pants, the score of the *St. Matthew Passion*, a few books, and a warm Australian wool robe, a present for Father from Martine.

A thin pink stripe appeared on the horizon.

Oh, everything was allowed at that moment, at that moment of return from the long, hard journey, after the long search, the long wait, and the ten-day ride on the freight train that brought them back. A freight train had taken them away and a freight train had brought them back. Everything was allowed at that moment of return from the journey from which it so often seemed they would not return. Such a moment deserves to be recorded exactly.

The city was dark. The square near the bridge, with its looming stone statues, was empty. The river below was silent and invisible. And the houses were dark.

A man she met on the bridge gave her directions. The third street to the right was called Lakowa Street, Meadow Street. Meadows, meadows . . . Did she really still believe in the magic of names and all those old superstitions? Shame, shame.

Oh, she wasn't ashamed of anything at that moment —nor was she at all sure that the magic had lost its power. She wasn't even ashamed of these "ohs" with which she now started her sentences and which she ordinarily took such pains to avoid.

At the corner were two street signs: the old German one said *Wiesenstrasse*. The new Polish one said *ul. Lakowa*. Meadow Street.

The street was wide and level. The buildings tall, with curved balconies and little tree-shaded lawns in front of their doors. Despite the darkness, everything was suddenly detailed, perfectly clear.

Number six, the third from the corner. Now she was running. On the fence in front of number six was a white sign. She knew what it said: Father's name, his office hours, from . . . till . . . From five to seven Father saw patients.

She sat down on the sidewalk and remained there, suddenly faint.

The pink stripe was glowing on the horizon, but the darkness still hung on. How silent it was! Everything in her fell silent and still. What peace . . .

She rose from the sidewalk, walked to the gate, rang the bell. After a long while she heard, inside the building, on the first floor, someone opening the door, asking who was ringing and what was the matter. It was Father's voice.

She answered, "It's us."

Her voice was weak, Father couldn't hear her. He asked if it was an emergency. For the second time, this time louder, she said, "It's us. It's us."

She heard him cry out. She heard his footsteps. He was running to the door.

Running, he called their names.

EPILOGUE

I remembered a circular plaza, but it turned out to be rectangular. It was hard to believe how different the plaza was, or rather, how my memory had changed it, giving it a different shape, generously adding trees, which in my memory were thickly planted but in fact were rather sparse.

It was also hard to believe that I sensed the plaza—round, not rectangular—before we reached the corner, although we were wandering blindly, without a city map, guided only by the trolley tracks. But before we reached the corner, I began to walk faster, and soon I was running.

It was a strange way to act, like a dog that's picked up a scent, and all the more strange, in that nothing was leading me on, not a single detail indicated that the plaza was nearby, and the surroundings—stores, shop windows, cafés—were completely unfamiliar, especially since they were all gaudily colored, so different from how they'd looked when the only color was gray, the cold gray of the stone.

"Here it is!" I cried, "Here it is!" and suddenly I was running.

The Journey

I ran into a woman carrying a bag of groceries. "Unheard of!" she yelled indignantly, and because B. just happened to click his camera at that moment, I have her indignation preserved on film, immortalized together with her face, her coarse, thick features.

She was right to be indignant. After all, who runs like that today on a crowded street, smacking into pedestrians, in broad daylight? Before . . . well, that was a different story. But today? What was surprising was the coincidence, that "Unheard of," said about me, just as it had been then, in the same town, in the same tone, and in both cases by a woman.

Once again I saw the stony face of the interpreter who heard my answer to the question and didn't translate it, but instead exclaimed, "Unheard of! You're lying!"

And she was right.

I stopped at the corner. It only took one look for me to realize that the place had changed its shape. I had expected it to be round, I had expected to find on my right the long gray stone building with the old wooden gate that the policeman opened for us and then closed. But, turning to the right, I saw only a tree, and under the tree, a bench, and on the bench an elderly woman with some needlework in her hand. A child was playing nearby. The long gray stone building was on the opposite side, at the far end of the plaza, behind some spindly trees. The thick, dome-like trees that shaded the entire plaza, and the green canopies under which we had strolled, tired and hungry and speaking Polish, had vanished as well.

The plaza was a rectangle. The building was on the opposite side. There were neither thick trees nor green canopies, just some thin trunks with few branches. B. clicked and clicked *to immortalize the plaza, and I kept saying, "This is it, this is it. Only it's completely different."*

I wanted everything to be like it had been. I wanted the square to become round and cover itself over with trees, and I wanted the gray stone building to return to its proper place. Then it was a sleepy, empty plaza; gravel crunched under our feet, and under the policeman's feet; there was not a soul around, just the three of us, as if we were on stage.

For thirty years the policeman had led us through the circular plaza with thick trees to the building on the right. From now on, was he going to lead us in a different direction? And through which plaza? Circular or rectangular? Thick trees or bare? And would I be troubled, knowing I'd remembered it wrong?

I approached the stone building reluctantly. Above the gate was a white sign. "School," read B., whose vision was better than mine.

They must have moved the police to a more modern building.

Suddenly the gate swung open on its own, and a middle-aged man in a navy striped suit appeared.

"Excuse me, please," said B. "Was this once a police station?"

The man looked at us, astonished.

"Ja . . . ja . . . That's right. During the war this was a police station, and afterwards as well, until 1950 . . ."

He was about to ask why we were interested in Hitler's police station, but I didn't feel like talking about it.

"Thank you," I said, coolly, and quickly walked in. Inside, the light was dim, just as it had been then; the wide,

*wooden stairs were the same ones we'd climbed with the po-
liceman behind us. Upstairs was the long, dark hallway with
doors on both sides. The walls were thick, the ceiling vaulted.
I hadn't noticed that.*

On the first door was a sign: TEACHERS ROOM. *This
was the room to which the policeman had led us. At the desk
sat a skinny, hawk-faced policeman, and by the wall, on chairs,
other policemen. Our entrance had interrupted a raucous conversation. They stared at us. The one with the hawk-face
squinted.*

*"Try it. Perhaps the room is open," suggested B. The
knob turned. We stood in the doorway.*

*The room was bright and spacious. In the middle was a
long, narrow table covered with green felt, surrounded by
chairs. By the door, where the desk had been, was a small,
round table and upholstered armchairs. There were begonias
on the windowsills—they had been empty before.*

*I could see the scene. We had been sitting on the right,
by the wall. The interpreter stood in front of us. She had just
begun to translate when she exclaimed, "Unheard of! You're
lying!" And she was right.*

*The hawk-faced policeman squinted at us and shouted,
"I'm calling the Gestapo!" and picked up the receiver and
dialed the number . . .*

*And just at that moment, the door, at which we now stood,
opened, and the short, fat station commander walked into the
room.*

*Our fate suddenly came to a halt and hung there for a
moment, suspended over the abyss it had been racing toward,*

hung there for a few minutes (five? six?) and then, just as suddenly, turned . . .

This was why I had come here, just for that moment at the crossroads, that sudden turn, that circus trick performed by our fate.

The rectangular plaza was bright with sunshine. The man in the dark suit paced beside the gate. He was waiting for us; he was curious. He asked whether we were satisfied with our inspection. We mumbled a polite reply.

"I speak Polish myself," he said suddenly; he almost sounded a little embarrassed. "I was brought here as a laborer, and I decided to stay. I got married. My wife is German. I work in the school as a watchman. I heard you speak Polish, so . . . Well, what is it like in Poland now?"

We explained that we left Poland many years ago, that we lived in Israel, that we were Jewish.

"And may I ask why you came here?" he gestured toward the school building.

"My wife was arrested here," said B. "She wanted to see . . ."

"And they let you go?"

"You might say that."

"Oh, you were very lucky." He nodded his head and peered at me nosily. "I used to work nearby, for a farmer. There were many Poles working here, and many other foreigners."

There were thin little trees on the rectangular plaza. Mothers were sitting on benches, children digging in the sand-box . . . In a moment it would turn out that he used to come to Olek's to play cards and listen to the patriotic poems Olek's wife used to recite.

"No, no . . . I wasn't here." We shook hands and said goodbye. He seemed moved by the encounter.

"Why didn't you tell him?" asked B. "I'm sure you would have found you had acquaintances in common."

"I've had enough."

On the other side of the plaza, I paused at the streetcar stop and looked to the right. The elderly woman sat on the bench with her needlework in her hand; a child played at her feet, while just behind her, the large gray stone building still hovered in the shadows of the thick, dome-like trees.